Bones to Biscuits
the dog foodbook

Linda McDonald is also author of:

Ice Cream, Sherbet, and Ices
Contact Lenses: How to Wear Them Successfully

Bones to Biscuits
the dog foodbook

Linda McDonald

Illustrations by David Barker

Oaklawn Press, Inc.
283 South Lake Avenue
Pasadena, California 91101
1977

Library of Congress Cataloging in Publication Data

McDonald, Linda
    Bones to biscuits.

    Includes index.
    1. Dogs—Food.   I. Title.
SF427.4.M38   636.7'08'55   77-1236
ISBN 0-916198-03-0

Oaklawn Press, Inc.
283 South Lake Avenue
Pasadena, California 91101

Illustrations by David Barker

Printed in the United States of America

This is for
Johann Magistrale
and
the other dogs next door

Contents

Foreword

Jo-Marie Sekol, D. V. M.
Doctor of Veterinary Medicine
Alhambra, California

Bones to Biscuits is a helpful guide to dog food preparation and feeding. It covers everything the pet owner needs to know about when, how and what to feed the family dog. Linda tells you how to choose and prepare regular commercial pet foods and how to use them in conjunction with home-made rations and table scraps. To form such a balanced diet all the necessary nutrients must be present in proper amounts and proper proportions. The diet should also supply enough energy to put these nutrients to work.

The advent of canned and dried foods has made it easy for pet owners to feed their dogs; but it should be noted that each type of food has its own shortcomings. There is a great variance in the quality of prepared foods and in the requirements essential to each dog. Each animal is an individual and although averages can be quoted, the main concern should be with the results and net amounts consumed. Know your pet; evaluate his condition and the amount he eats, and his optimum weight. Nothing will improve your dog's health or increase his lifespan as much as a balanced diet.

Bones to Biscuits is divided into several sections, each of which deals with a specific area of canine nutrition. If you prefer a home-made ration, or it is a necessity, Linda has provided mixtures and variety for all breeds. There is also useful information for new puppy owners. Growing pups need two and one-half times more energy than adults. Malnutrition is a major cause of puppy mortality, and needs particular attention.

The information in the chapter called "Special Diets" is helpful to dog owners with pets having special health requirements. These problems include impaired kidney function, heart disease, allergy, obesity, and intestinal disorders.

After reading what follows the pet owner should have a better idea of what his pet requires to lead a healthy, long life.

Bones to Biscuits
the dog foodbook

1. Your Dog's Food

"Are you hungry Dutchess? Would you like a savory stew? Or some meatballs? Or some yummies?" How often have you heard this or similar variations as a receptive pet wagged his tail in wild anticipation of what was to follow?

What kind of dog food is right for your dog has become as intriguing as the number of dog breeds; because one deals not only with dogs, but with the people who own and feed them. And, as the animal population continues to grow at a pace ten times faster than humans, there will be more ideas tossed around about what pets should and should not eat. In terms of food, that means a lot of eating.

You can talk to dozens of people and you will find that no two feed their dogs in exactly the same way, but almost any of them could show you dogs in apparent good health.

There are people who insist on boiled potatoes in their skins mixed with hamburger and alfalfa meal as the only dog food. Some believe in a diet of meat, milk, and vegetables; others insist on stale bread, cooked eggs, and meat; and still other dogs are fed a mixture of dry meal and meat, horse meat and corn meal, or fish and cooked grain. Then there are breeders who don't believe in feeding milk or vegetables.

On the other hand, some breeders' dogs are strict vegetarians. One couple who raises show dogs make their own special ration every two weeks. It consists of soybeans, bran, wheat germ, cooked rice and vegetables, tomato juice, kibble and vitamins.

After all the points of view on the subject have been aired and argued, one fact remains: The dog's digestive system is a fairly tolerant apparatus and it is more than likely that he can be kept in peak condition on any one of several diets if the owner just uses a little common sense.

Feeding a dog can be simple or complicated. Or as glamorous as the master chooses to make it. However, the real experts—breeders and veterinarians—agree that certain elements must be present and that correct feeding is of prime importance in raising a healthy dog.

Genetics and environment are two other important factors which contribute to the overall health of your pet. But adequate and balanced nutrition is what enables your dog to arrive at his inherited potential. Disposition, appearance, growth and length of life depend on the food you give him.

It is difficult to establish just how much every dog needs to eat. Each dog is an individual. An inactive house pet needs less food than a growing puppy or a dog that gets hard exercise, or one that is kept outside in a cold climate, or a female nursing puppies. Growing pups require more food than adult dogs, the amount of course, depending upon the individual puppy and his rate of growth.

One is liable to think of both dogs and cats as carnivorous animals since their teeth are well-adapted to tearing and puncturing flesh. It is incorrect to classify our little friends this way; both are omnivores since they live both on vegetable matter and meat.

In the wild state ancestors of all dogs preyed upon other animals for food: They ate as much of their prey as possible, generally beginning with the stomach and intestinal contents first to obtain partially digested grains and vegetables, which provided carbohydrates, vitamins, minerals and fiber. Last, they ate the muscle tissue, which we refer to as meat, to get their protein.

It is very unlikely that any of our pets of today, or yesterday, could live for very long on meat alone without developing deficiency disease. To maintain optimum health a 100 percent meat diet is not recommended. A dog needs carbohydrates, vitamins and minerals along with his protein and fat to make a complete and balanced diet.

Dog owners are hurting their pets by believing they can feed all-meat diets. Animal studies have been conducted using all meat and meat by-products as the sole food. All-meat diets give the animal 40 percent of its calories from protein and 60 percent from fat with almost none from carbohydrates. If used exclusively such a diet has harmful effects on dogs. Dogs cannot use this large amount of protein without causing the liver and kidneys to become overworked.

Dogs should not be fed wholly on soft food either; this causes the teeth to accumulate tartar. Badly affected teeth become disfigured, may fall out, or have to be extracted.

Dogs that are fed complete and balanced diets do not need vitamin supplements. In the case of a pregnant dog, over-supplementation can cause serious problems, birth defects being the most serious. Don't feed a dog cat food either, since cat food cannot supply a dog's needs.

Another misconception is that raw eggs are a dietary bonus; that they will make a dog's coat glisten. Actually, the reverse is true. Too many raw eggs can cause biotin deficiency which in turn may lead to dermatitis and loss of hair. Avidin, an enzyme found in egg whites, destroys the vitamin, biotin. Raw or cooked "yolk" is all right. But to be on the safe side, eggs, when they are fed, should always be cooked.

Dogs, like humans, need a balanced diet. Major manufacturers of dog food frequently imply in their advertisements that all-meat products are best for dogs because dogs are carnivores. This is not true, however, since dogs are omnivores. Dogs eat and like fruits, vegetables and cereals as well as meat, and prefer this combination to an all-meat diet.

The National Academy of Science's National Research Council recommends that dogs get 20 to 25 percent of their calories from protein, 20 to 30 percent from fat, and the rest from carbohydrates.

One leading veterinarian claims that dogs can manage nicely on 14 percent protein (dry basis) as a minimum, 20 percent fat, and the rest carbohydrate.

Recently the Federal Trade Commission ordered manufacturers of pet foods to back up advertising claims of their products. One major food producer claimed that its food provided a complete and balanced diet with all the vitamins and minerals needed by a dog, with the product being composed wholly of meat and meat by-products. This, among others, was a typical example of a pet food advertisement for which substantiation was demanded.

Today, pet foods are even artificially colored to give the appearance of meat and gravy and to make the grain content resemble meat. As far as red food coloring is concerned the FDA has banned dyes Nos. 2 and 4. The last red dye still on the market is Red No. 40, which two scientists and a medical school professor say causes cancer and should be banned immediately. One of these people, who is convinced the dye is a carcinogen, is a veterinary pathologist in the FDA's Bureau of Drugs. Another doctor, affiliated with the Center for Science in the Public Interest, states that "artificial colors are the most hazardous category of food additives." He goes on to say, "The public should stay away from colors on its own. Artificial colors are almost always listed on labels of foods. People should just stop buying them and stop feeding them to their families."

The next time you buy pet food read the label. Artificial coloring serves no purpose other than to make the product look better to the human purchaser rather than to make the dog healthy or happy. Since dogs are pretty much color blind, color is not important in the selection of dog food.

According to a survey by the U.S. Disease Control Center at least one million people in this country are bitten by dogs every year. Other authorities think the figure should be doubled. Statistics in New York City between 1965 and 1972 give 3 to 7 p.m. as the most likely time for dog bites. Interestingly, this time period coincides with the time pet owners usually feed their pets.

It is true that more dogs than ever are playing guard in households: But another explanation for this aggressive behavior may be related to chemical additives in commercial pet foods. Some readers may be familiar with a book by a leading pediatrician that attributes hyperactivity in children to the preservatives and artificial food colorings in processed foods. Perhaps there is a correlation too between what a dog eats and temperament changes, including biting. Whatever the cause of excited or aggressive dogs, it should be noted that health food stores are now distributing pet foods with *no* preservatives and *no* artificial food colorings.

One food editor for a leading newspaper went as far as to rate about a dozen types of dog food according to taste. The author of this book also sampled dog food and made her own observations regarding consistency and odor. Some of a variety of flavor and texture defects we both noted were a consistency similar to cold cream, a stale biscuit texture, mushy texture and no seasoning, a gooey texture, a good odor but no taste, a rubbery and tasteless sensation, a flavor sweet like pastry, or strong like burnt processed cheese, or with a slight odor of decayed grass, charcoal-flavored biscuits with an asphalt odor, some food having a pasty appearance (and taste) and a drastically red color, some with awful appearance and foul taste, others with a strong mysterious odor, smoked flavor, dry like sawdust, and a crunch that was similar to chewing mashed nuts, shells and all.

Dogs, like humans, are aware of the wide span of tastes and textures in prepared foods. But unlike humans they cannot communicate their likes and dislikes.

Numerous preservatives are used in pet foods to prevent spoilage. Nutrient additives go into the ingredients as occasionally do drugs. It's up to the individual pet owner whether or not he wants his dog to ingest these materials.

Diethylcarbamazine, a drug used to control large round worms in dogs, is added to some brands of pet food. In the past, a particular dog food was labled as containing methyltestosterone. The food was intended for consumption by guard dogs, to increase aggressiveness.

In semi-moist dog food, potassium sorbate is added to insure long-term room temperature stability against mold growth. Propylene glycol provides some additional protection and contributes to produce a moist chewy texture. These ingredients help the product retain adequate stability even if the package is opened and subsequently reclosed. For more information on stabilizers see the section on Soft-Moist Foods in Chapter 2.

Have you ever read the label on Beef Stew? The ingredients listed suggest a concentrated chemical diet for dogs rather than stew.

> Meat by-products, beef, soy flour, carrots, potatoes, salt, soybean oil, potassium chloride, guar gum, vitamin A palmitate (stability improved), D-activated animal sterol (source of vitamin D_3), DL-alpha tocopheryl acetate (source of vitamin E), vitamin B_{12} supplement, choline chloride, BHT (a preservative), citric acid, methionine magnesium oxide, manganous oxide, iron (ferrous), sulfate, copper oxide, zinc oxide, cobalt carbonate, ethylene diamine dihydroiodide, charcoal, sodium nitrite, caramel color, artificial color and water sufficient for processing has been added.

If given a choice, would dogs really prefer this concentrated and processed ration to a freshly made one with more bulk and flavor than the commercial variety? Probably not.

The additives and preservatives in commercial dog foods may cause allergic reactions in some dogs. When you buy commercial foods you should be aware that they vary markedly in nutrient quality and in supplements. Always read the label on any food you purchase for your dog. And report to the Federal Drug Administration any false claims by pet food companies, the illegal use of drugs, or other materials that could be hazardous to your pet's health.

The shelves in grocery stores are brimming with pet foods that claim to be a complete and balanced diet for an animal. Some of them may be well-balanced, wholesome foods; but there are others whose nutritional value is deficient.

Researchers have tested scores of these foods and found that some were deficient in as many as six essential nutrients. Even though these foods were deficient they were eagerly accepted by dogs. So acceptance is no guide to the completeness of a food.

Unless pet foods are properly stored and used relatively soon the vitamin and mineral supplements they contain will deteriorate.

When you see the term "complete and balanced diet" on a pet food label, this does not mean that the food can be used as the sole diet for every dog. What it really means is that the product is a "maintenance diet." In other words the product provides the minimum diet to assure that the dog will maintain his size and weight. Growing dogs, pregnant dogs, ones nursing puppies, and dogs under stress all need more nutrients than a "maintenance diet" can provide. A "complete and balanced diet" for one dog may be an incomplete and unbalanced diet for another.

Because many dog owners are sometimes unaware of their pets' dietary needs, veterinarians have reported an increasing number of pets with nutritional deficiencies. Ask any veterinarian. He'll tell you that he regularly sees pets suffering from the same basic malady—diet deficiencies. They are afflicted with many ailments: Respiratory infections, weakness, sparse coat, eye infections, skin lesions, dry and itching skin, deformed ribs, poor growth, rickets, anemia, diarrhea, reproductive disorders, urinary defects, deafness, restlessness, bad breath, and inflamed looking gums and tongues. These are not isolated cases. Veterinarians treat many animals on a regular basis with these conditions. So you can see why they have a healthy skepticism regarding the claims by commercial dog-food makers, which tout their rations as supposedly providing a "complete and balanced diet" for dogs.

Some veterinarians encourage pet owners to supplement commercial food with table scraps, fat and meat trimmings. In particular, they encourage it with hunting and lactating dogs to keep the animals in top shape. What the professionals are opposed to, however, is indiscriminate supplementations, particularly vitamins and minerals, by people who don't understand why they are doing it.

A pet food label which indicates that all the nutrients are included for balanced nutrition is no safeguard. Deficiencies almost invariably result when some brands are fed as an exclusive diet. The reason for this is that certain food elements are not present in forms that can be readily assimilated by the pet's digestive system.

A good example is the protein in beef by-products. Gristle, hair, hooves, lungs and tails are all protein; but they cannot be transformed into nourishment by the pet! The same is true of some carbohydrates. These may be just so much indigestible cellulose—the by-products of cereals and other foods that manufacturers find unsuitable for human consumption. Fats may also be worthless mineral compounds. How can the pet owner be certain his dog's system will assimilate the nutrients in these by-products?

Even though a dog may readily accept concentrated nutrients will he thrive on them? Is this the best way, in the long run, to meet his caloric demands? What about the dog which exceeds the recommended daily ration? What about the dog which doesn't assimilate the nutrients? Or the one which needs additional bulk in the diet?

From the beginning of time the average pet has lived largely on whatever was left over from the table and what he could forage around the countryside. He appeared to get along nicely on remnant meat and scraps. Today, few of the dogs in France are given commercially prepared pet food; they get along on table scraps and love it.

Basically speaking, what dogs have eaten since the dawn of civilization pretty well coincided with the diet of their owners. And to some extent dogs have suffered from the same ups and downs and maladies their masters have. Therefore, it would not seem unreasonable to contend that you may feed a dog, within reason, almost anything a human would eat.

During the Depression era, when dogs were not hampered by leash laws, they supplemented their table scraps from neighborhood dumps, or garbage cans, or by hunting rodents and small animals. In his natural state the dog made some attempt to balance his diet. Then, toward the middle of this century, manufacturers of cereals and other foods found it profitable to use their by-products in pet foods. At this time the first scientific attempt was made to establish the nutrient requirement of dogs. When this happened it became the "in" thing for dogs to eat processed packaged foods. Whether or not this has enhanced the lifespan of the animal is another question.

Once processed dog food reached its peak in popularity, dog food companies looked for new ways to boost sales. They came up with food variations for every need. Now there are some fifteen thousand labels from which to choose. There are prescription diets to treat dogs with diabetes, colitis, hepatitis, food allergies, heart, kidney, and liver conditions, and dermatoses. Since about 41 percent of American dogs are overweight from eating too much processed pet food, the pet food merchandisers have had to develop low-calorie foods to relieve dogs of their obesity. There are special foods for growing puppies and pregnant and aging dogs too. There are even foods with a higher palatability than regular foods to tempt the fussy dog, which isn't allowed to get hungry, or lacks the stimulus to eat what's put before him.

Today, Americans spend $2.5 billion a year on commercially prepared pet food. This is more than six times as much as they spend on baby food. And pet owners may very well match this amount with other products and services they lavish on pets.

Research has shown that pet supplies are primarily impulse items and that sales of flea collars, leashes and bowls lead to one or more sales of other items during the same shopping trip. Among them: brushes, combs, chains, blankets, sweaters, neckties, "poochy" coats, raincoats, boots, collars, beds, carriers, name plates, shampoos, hair dryers, perfumes, soaps, edible toys and vitamins. Don't overlook the amount spent on license fees, animal pound fees, dental, veterinary and grooming care and pet walkers and sitters, eyeglasses, sun lenses, contact lenses, and shiny black granite headstones for departed pets.

There are also doggie psychologists, psychiatrists, psychics, astrologers, dermatologists, pathologists, radiologists, acupuncturists, body massagers, trainers, and gourmet butchers. To this you can add doggie health spas, hotels, ranches, cemeteries and crematories, pet health insurance and dog intelligence tests.

In the United States 2,000 dogs and cats are born every hour while only 415 babies are. Although figures on animal population vary it is believed that there are about 64.4 million dogs and cats that are pets. There are another 80 to 100 million strays or abandoned dogs in the United States. The billions of dollars spent on these animals well exceed the gross national product of entire nations. And it shows little sign of letting up. What is spent on the luxury items alone would feed millions and millions of starving people throughout the world.

Pet-food manufacturers spend $165 million annually on advertising aimed, of course, at the pet owner. Look at the colorfully packaged items displayed in the aisles of your supermarket. Or, turn on your television set. Puppies tumble over each other fumbling to get their morning tidbits. Fullgrown dogs race hungrily across the kitchen to gulp down a full bowl of their own special food.

In pet-food commercials the pets are even taking on the attributes of humans and are shown addressing the viewer directly on their own behalf. The animals converse with each other and engage in all sorts of other behavior that is exclusively human. For example, dogs are shown responding to on-the-air interviews on the subject of dog dinners. One of the ads goes something like this: A dog, asked to comment on his taste preferences, exclaims in a doggy voice, "I think [Dry Chow's] richer flavor is definitely richer." Another dog, when asked to comment, observes that [Dry Chow's] heavy on nutrition man!" And another exclaims enthusiastically, "Uh, the new, richer flavor—superb!"

In another commercial the master of ceremonies asks an assembly of dogs how they feel about a particular brand of dry dog food. The dogs respond by raising their right paws in approval, exclaiming "Uh huh, yeah." In the next scene they clap their doggy paws together in a round of applause to show their enthusiasm for the new dry food.

Another commercial shows a dog wearing glasses quietly reading a book before he is interrupted by a call to dinner. Not only have the pets become literate and assumed human characteristics, but human beings have been metamorphosized into dogs.

In one commercial, women are depicted in a kitchen scene wearing dog costumes speaking to each other through large dogs' heads. The dog-woman skit goes approximately like this: A dog, who lives next door, has just dropped in to borrow some food. In a worrisome voice she woofs, "Oh, Marge, Harry's boss is coming for dinner and I ran out of food." The other "dog-woman" helpfully puts her paws on a package of dry food that she's certain will impress Harry's boss. Next comes a petorama of "dog people" gathered around the table, Harry's boss included. The boss proceeds to compliment the hostess in a bowwow voice, "Hmm! This [dinner] is delicious, crunchy dry!" Harry agrees and declares through his "dog's head" that his dinner is also "delicious with its gravy too."

Other numerous examples can be found by looking over any woman's magazines. ". . . all he ever eats is canned dog food. It's got to be moist and meaty, or he just stares at you and walks away. So if it doesn't come from a can, forget it."

It is evident that the pet owner is being brainwashed by the pet-food manufacturer which is highly motivated to sell its product. What is so ironic about this type of advertising is that pet food manufacturers also claim that dry, kibbled food meets all the nutritional requirements of dogs without requiring meatier substances.

This same manufacturer, cited above, which was promoting dog burgers in the advertisement, makes this notation on the package of a dry chunk style food it sells: "provides a normal, healthy dog with a complete balanced diet, including all the nutrition your dog is known to need."

You'll also come across such catchy phrases as: "Some real cheese taste, plus more meat." "A quarter egg in every burger." "Half an egg in every pouch. Three eggs in every six-pack." "The canned dog food without the can." "He'll love the taste; you'll love the smell; you'll both love it." "The balanced dinner Lassie eats." "The protein plate for dogs." "They're crisp and crunchy hot dog shaped treats with a zesty cheese flavor . . . your dog will flip over 'em." "Lets you feed your dog like a member of the family." "Carefully broiled to a sharp-shooting perfection." "Satisfy the cheese hound in your dog." "Our burger is better for your dog than hamburger."

All of these well turned phrases, coupled with scenes of dogs and puppies in adorable tail-wagging action, happily gobbling down food, not only help persuade pet owners to buy products but may even influence many people to go out and buy pets to consume the pet food being advertised.

Pets are eating better than ever before. When you read the labels on cans it's easy to get the impression that the food is suitable for human consumption. You'll come across "Chunky Beef with Eggs and Cheese," "Chunky Chicken Dinner," "Cheese Burger," "Super Meat Loaf," "Ranch Style Dinner," "Chicken and Gravy," "Chicken Stew," "Beef Stew," and "Chuck Wagon Stew." There are even crackers shaped like people with the slogan "Give your dog a little somebody between meals."

The advertising is indeed effective. People all over brag about the brand they feed their dogs. If your taste buds are not aroused by all the tantalizing flavors then perhaps you'll get hooked on the items offered for sale on the package. If you turn in the price spot and a check or money order you can obtain such things as lace tablecloths, pearl necklaces, a sportsman's all-purpose knife or a new feeding dish.

Dog food has become well-nigh irresistible. And the ever-increasing consumption of these "gourmet" foods for dogs results from the pet owners' desire to do the "novel"—to use the products that have been made readily available.

All of these foods come in appetizing packages designed more to tempt you than your dog. They appeal to your taste for meat, cheese, eggs, sauces and gravies. The advertising is selling you, not your pet.

One major producer of dog food promoted its product with the intention of persuading dog owners, who bought the far cheaper brands of dry food, to become "classier" and switch to buying the more expensive brand. The claim made on national television implied that the higher priced food provided superior nutrition and was more appealing to dogs than the lower priced food.

Television viewers became so impressed with the virtues of high-priced dog food that they avoided buying the cheaper brands, which they thought might be inferior in quality. High-priced dog food became a status symbol. The social status of people could now be judged by the expensiveness of the dog food they bought. It wasn't long before the producers of the cheaper brands were forced to raise the price of their products to keep potential customers interested.

The manufacturer of one high-priced brand went as far as to convey the company's view of the "cheaper" food. The company told supermarket operators throughout the country "you make more profit per can on [our food], so the more space you give to high-profit [food] the more money you'll make." This is how the "super" premium priced dog food replaced the cheaper priced foods on your supermarket shelf.

As other manufacturers developed premium foods they made such claims as: "so good, dogs chose it six to one in a recent test over leading competitive varieties." Another manufacturer which put out a premium priced canned food claimed that its product "tastes better than any canned dog food."

When the newly developed semi-moist foods came out they were advertised with such slogans as "the canned dog food without the can," "Dogs think it's meat, but it's more," and "More nourishing than the sirloin steak you'd eat yourself."

While still new, competitors with meat products started striking back at the semi-moist dog food campaigns, warning dog owners that their all-meat product had "No sugar added," and that semi-moist:

> Burger dog foods . . . can contain as much as twenty per cent sugar. There's also up to thirty-five per cent vegetable matter. How much real beef, or meat by-products are in a burger? Well, it would take at least ten burgers to equal the beef and meat by-products in one can of . . . Beef.

The introduction of semi-moist products led to a kind of "gas war" in dog-food promotion. The meat competitors launched an all-out attack against the moist products because the latter contained sucrose. Then it wasn't long before veterinarians and professional dog breeders started to criticize all-meat diets saying they might have adverse effects on animals' health.

The F.T.C. eventually stepped in and required that a producer of all-meat canned food change its slogan from "Your dog needs meat" to "your dog *loves* meat." So successful was the promotion that one producer of all-meat canned food increased his sales from sixteen million dollars a year to a hundred and twenty-five million dollars. Fortunately F.T.C. intervention helped nullify the effects of ad campaigns against semi-moist products.

Pet food advertisers and manufacturers have commissioned studies to ascertain the buying habits and attitudes of owners toward their pets. Marketing research shows that it's the family who may buy the dog but it's the woman who picks up the food at the supermarket and feeds the dog. She is the one the pet-food people watch. It's her attitudes, buying habits and motivations that are studied with care.

One reporter who examined these studies noted that it is primarily women who receive satisfaction and emotional support from their pets. When the man of the house is gone the dog is something else from which affection can be received. In these studies the following terms and phrases were used: "surrogate child," "ego-gratification," "love object," "totally involving kind of love," and "eager for bodily contact." A psychiatrist is needed to explain the relationships in more detail.

It's not the pet which watches the television commercials, nor is it the pet which selects the new flavor on the supermarket shelf, which determines the content of commercial dog food flavors. New pet-food flavors are tested on pet owners rather than pets. "Real cheese taste," "Cheese Burger," "Chicken Dinner," "Beef Stew," "Meat Loaf," and other humanized varieties that emphasize the delectability of human food evoke the salivary response of the pet food purchaser. What a treat! Her dog is going to love her more if she buys food that tastes like stews, casseroles, meat loaf, and chicken and dumplings.

This is all very thought-provoking. It raises the issue whether the lady in the house, with the help of incessant advertising campaigns, is being conditioned and trained to follow the bidding of the pet food merchandisers.

The infiltration of animals in commercials, and the use of animals in films is of particular interest in that their use has necessitated an animal control bill. Note the work being done by the Humane Society of the United States as regards animal mistreatment in the motion picture-television industry. During the filming of pet food commercials undercover informants have reported incidents in which animals were not fed, worked in hot temperatures, and kept in cramped cages. There is little if any veterinary care for these animals and many of them are believed to get viruses and die. But there is no way to know for sure because inventories are not kept. Investigators are reluctant to name manufacturers of pet food commercials allegedly involved until they have finished collecting evidence. The Humane Society, however, is considering legal action against them. The problem has gained enough attention so that national humane groups are planning to ask Congress and legislatures in the states to adopt laws to punish cruelty to animals in films.

All in all, pet food promotion has become a game. Millions of dollars are spent annually on advertising that disparages, steals away or expands major markets. All kinds of weaponry to outdo one another, from television commercials to free coupons and magazine ads, have been employed by the industry's giants to make sales gains and halt the growth of competitors. As one pet food advertising agency put it, "Meat! Meat is the name of the game."

Just because commercially prepared foods are enticingly advertised and readily available is no reason to stuff and overfeed our dogs with high protein foods. Our main goal in feeding them should be sound nutrition—not necessarily super-nutrition. We're not competing in a race to grow stronger and stronger dogs. Less emphasis should be placed on competitiveness and more emphasis on what is nutritionally adequate for a dog at a relatively low price.

2. Commercial Dog Food

Commercially prepared dog food can be divided into three general categories; 1. dry food, 2. soft-moist food, and 3. canned food. These are the most popular dog foods; however, fresh or frozen meat and meat by-products are also widely available and used by pet owners.

If you prefer to use a commercial food in conjunction with homemade formulas, decide on the diet that is most convenient for you to prepare, and then stick with it. When an animal's diet is frequently changed it can cause digestive upsets and vitamin and mineral imbalances.

This does not mean that you should not vary the proteins, cereals and vegetables in a home ration. This type of variety is good because no one food supplies all needed nutrients in sufficient amounts. For good nutrition all of the essential food elements must work together. Therefore, well balanced nutrition calls for a well chosen variety of foods. Variety is the best way to prevent vitamin and mineral deficiencies.

Preventing deficiencies works the same way with dogs as with human beings. If either were regularly to consume certain limited foods there's a good chance one or more essential nutrients would be missing from the diet. If this nutrient is missing from the diet over very long periods of time, "deficiency diseases" such as rickets, scurvy, or certain anemias may develop.

Variety is also preferable if you travel around a lot with your dog because there is less of a chance for stomach or bowel problems to crop up. Upsets are surely to occur with even the most minor change in a ration if the dog is accustomed to eating the same food every day. The thing you want to avoid, above all, is switching about erratically from dry to canned food or dry to home rations every other week. It's this type of variety that causes problems.

You should also know that some chain supermarkets put out their own brand names of pet food. These private labels are often duplications of national brands. Generally speaking they are equal in quality to the name brands and often cheaper to buy. Pet owners are switching more and more to these house brands.

Large markets frequently sell two brands of dog food made by one packer from the same formula. If you buy commercial food on the basis of what might appeal to your dog, chances are you may buy two brands to see which one your dog prefers. You may offer one of the brands in the morning only to have your dog leave it. In the evening you offer the other brand, and the dog, hungry by this time, gulps it down, so you think the second brand is superior to the first brand. Actually, this is no test at all because what your dog ate may have been the same food you offered him in the morning. It could have been the same formula made by the same manufacturer, but packaged under a different label.

When shopping around be wary of bargain-priced brands of dog food ground up at the local feed mill. The quality of the grain may be poor and the ingredients used may not be present in the proper proportions. Cheap dog foods do not slide out of the can easily. They're somewhat more gummy than expensive brands and usually stick to the spoon or fork. They may even be improperly prepared, making the food unpalatable and unnourishing.

The most popular commercial dog foods are: dry foods, biscuits, soft-moist foods and canned foods.

Dry Foods

Dog pellets and dog meal differ only in form. Both foods contain the same assortment and quantities of nutrients and both may be fed interchangeably. They usually consist of about half cereal ingredients and half animal proteins. They often include corn flakes, wheat flakes, soybean meal, peanut meal and bread meal. Crumbs and broken biscuits left over from the manufacturers of dog biscuits are included. And so are raw cereal products such as middlings. Occasionally, cheap flour is thrown in.

Animal proteins come from meat scraps and by-products, organs, fish meal, liver meal, skim milk powder and other such things. Vitamins and minerals are then added to make up for any imbalances in the mixture.

According to the manufacturer, either pellets or meal, can be used as a complete and total diet without supplements, although the use of meat, fish, cereals, or vegetables will add fiber and variety to the diet. When purchasing cereal-based dry dog food read the label carefully. Dry foods that don't contain a speck of meat may be described on the package as "meaty, juicy, and chunky."

Dry foods are usually low in fat content even though they are called "complete" foods. Most labels list a standardized protein and fat content. Check the "guaranteed analysis." Dry foods should include an animal protein source, such as meat meal, among its first three ingredients. The food should also have at least one cereal grain in its ingredients. One veterinarian states dry food should also contain fat in quantities not less than 7 percent per pound of dry matter.

There is great variance of opinion concerning the minimal fat requirements essential to each dog. The "guaranteed analysis" varies greatly from brand to brand. Read labels carefully for fat content.

Bacon drippings, chicken fat, roasting fat, lard, butter, or vegetable oil can be mixed with the dry food. For house dogs, some veterinarians recommend that 1 part fat be mixed with 4 parts of dry food. Active dogs require more fat.

Dry food has excellent storage characteristics due in part to its low fat content. Since it's easy to store, dry food permits the use of relatively inexpensive packaging techniques. However, the palatability is poor and in many cases, dogs refuse to eat it unless liquid is added prior to consumption. Adding liquid doesn't always solve the problem either since the food becomes mushy or doughy and is still refused by the dog if any other foods are around.

Dry food is available in three forms—bite size, meal form and chunk size. Bite size, which is also known as kibble, comes in easy-to-eat pieces. Either kibble or baked food is similar in density to a hard, baked dog biscuit. Few firms manufacture kibble because of the high cost.

Kibble is so tightly packed and baked that a dog receives the maximum amount of nutrition with a minimum amount of volume. It's chewy and crunchy and can be fed dry or moistened. Bite size is perfect for self-feeding as it ensures continual food intake.

Meal form should be fed while fresh and moistened with warm liquid. Chunk size should be fed dry right from the bag. Larger dogs usually like to crunch on this. Some dry foods are for puppies only. Some dry foods are specially prepared to form a gravy when water is added. But whether dogs really notice the difference between gravied or ungravied dog meal is difficult to determine.

Other than this there isn't too much difference between all of these dry foods. They are a mixture of homogenized meal, puffed and baked with a surrounding layer of fat. It is sometimes referred to as an extruded dog food. Kibble, however, does not fall into this category. Some dogs will not eat kibble as readily as an extruded dog food.

Most dry food has a combination of animal fat and soy bean oil which helps to make it palatable and insures that the dog has some fat for his caloric needs and nutritional requirements. This thin layer of fat, which appears invisible upon examination, is extremely important because it is necessary to hold the particles of food together. If this layer of fat were missing the food would crumble.

Meal-type food contains about 90 percent solids and 10 percent moisture. They supply 300-400 calories per cup, depending on the density of meal. They vary in quality and cost. All dry foods may be alternated in any of a number of ways. You can feed pellets one week and meal the next. Some owners feed pellets in the morning and meal in the evening. The meal provides a bulky soft diet, while the pellets provide crunch and exercise for the teeth and gums.

If you exercise your dog hard or use him for hunting get the brand of dry food that has the highest percentage of protein and fat listed on the label.

Pet owners who have trouble stimulating their dog's appetite may want to try changing from one dry food to another. This may encourage eating in the same way as an actual change of diet. Many pet owners have the impression that dry foods are cereals and canned foods are all meat. Canned and dry foods both contain meat proteins, but in the case of dry foods the water has been removed. Most pet owners are aware that a pound of dry food mixed with water goes a bit farther for their money than a pound of the ready-to-eat canned food.

It should be noted that "high protein" dry foods and "high protein" canned foods may cause severe diarrhea in some animals. These higher-priced, high protein products are sometimes more readily displayed in the fall hunting season, when hunters pay extra attention to their field dog's diet.

Biscuits

Biscuits also belong in the category of dry food. They come in many sizes, shapes, flavors and colors. Some common flavors are meat, milk, liver, cheese, poultry and vegetable. Another variety combines meat and vegetable proteins with cheese, charcoal and ginger.

Most dog biscuits are fed as occasional snacks or training treats. Feeding too many may cause constipation and obesity. Too many biscuits also spoil the appetite for more complete foods essential for good health.

At one time dogs were reported to have fits and some forms of paralysis attributable to too many biscuits made from bleached flour. Biscuits are helpful in scraping off tooth tartar; They also encourage the development of strong gums and jaws.

Dog biscuits do not constitute a complete diet by any means. They can be used as a basic food, however, along with meat, fat, and vegetables. Some manufacturers claim their dog biscuits are nutritionally complete and can be fed as the sole diet. Researchers disagree with this because dog biscuits are composed mostly of second-grade wheat flour. However, the baking process by which they are manufactured exposes the nutrients to high heat, destroying some of the vitamins and amino acids. Also, due to the baking process, biscuits have a moisture content of about 7 percent. Always have plenty of fresh water available when an animal is fed biscuits.

Soft-Moist Foods

According to the maker, soft-moist foods, also known as burgers and patties, usually can be fed throughout a dog's life as the sole ration, except, perhaps in the instance of very large breeds. Soft-moist foods are a highly concentrated nutrient source with a solids content of about 75 percent and a moisture content of 25 percent.

They have a meat-like appearance, color, consistency and texture and are particularly characterized by their meat-like chewiness. They contain numerous additives so read the label carefully.

Soft-moist foods need no refrigeration. Under normal conditions they can be stored six months or longer without deterioration or changes in texture and color. These burgers and patties have been so heavily preserved that they can even be stored in an open unpackaged condition without spoiling.

The reason they keep so well is that such materials as sorbitol, propylene glycol, and sodium chloride are added to the ingredients or the packaging to prevent yeast and mold growth. These materials serve as texturizers too in that they help make the product soft and tender. Potassium sorbate as well as sorbic acid are also used either separately or in combination. The manner in which these agents are used varies considerably. They can be incorporated with the ingredients processed, others can be sprayed or coated on the surface of the product, and still others can be applied to the packaging which touches the product.

Technology has become so advanced that products resembling marbled meat can be produced. In other words, the patty will have a fat-like white portion randomly distributed in the red portion. Cuts resembling steaks and chops can be created by slicing through a loaf or roll that has a prefabricated bone-like structure.

These products are basically processed in this way; Chopped meat by-products are pasteurized in a combination with an emulsifier and all liquid ingredients at a high temperature for about 10 minutes. Next, colors, preservatives, crystalization retardant, flavors and nutrients are added. Following this comes the rest of the dry ingredients such as bone meal, soy flakes, soy hulls, dry skimmed milk and sugar. The final product is then cooked for about 7 more minutes, cooled, and packaged.

The fat content of soft-moist foods is derived from animal and vegetable sources. Some of these products are supposed to contain more protein than fresh hamburger meat. The more recent ones have their flavor enhanced with eggs and cheese. And the manufacturers often claim these foods will provide a total diet without protein supplementation.

Soft-moist foods are very dense, however, so follow package directions exactly to avoid overfeeding. Two 3-ounce patties are equal in feeding value to a 16-ounce can of pet food. Dry and soft-moist types can be combined to help increase the palatability of dry foods. These combinations are also helpful when feeding large breeds.

Whenever offering soft-moist foods always be certain that fresh water is available in a separate dish. Have it continually available in unlimited quantities. Water is extremely crucial to dogs on dense rations.

When soft-moist foods are fed as the sole ration it is recommended that you watch your dog's condition. If he maintains his weight and keeps active, is playful and good natured, you can be quite sure his food is agreeable. On the other hand, if he shows signs of irritability, has digestive upsets or experiences changes in temperament, your pet may be having a reaction to the chemical additives in soft-moist foods.

Canned Foods

There are two basic kinds of canned foods, all-meat canned foods and complete canned foods. The complete canned food consists of meat, fish or poultry products mixed with meal. It contains one or more vegetable protein sources as well as combinations of these, together with other nutritional supplements.

The all-meat kind, which is usually priced considerably higher than complete food, should be used with cereal and vegetables or a good dry meal. It's packed as all-chicken, all-liver, all-beef, all-horsemeat, etc. The makers of some canned meat add vitamins and minerals to enhance its nutritive value.

These special packs vary greatly in the quality of their protein. Never feed them to an animal as a complete diet. All-meat canned foods contain about 25 percent food solids and 75 percent moisture. Canned foods, unlike semi-moist foods, have the appearance of greater quantity because the moisture content is high.

Canned foods are referred to in the trade as "pudding foods." They are like a thick soup when poured into a can but contain gelatin to make a solid mass after processing. During the packing process the ingredients have to be sufficiently fluid to be pumped through the pipes leading to the filling lines. So the inclusion of gelatin in canned foods permits a semisolid appearance in the presence of high water content.

Always read the label on canned food. It will state whether it is a complete, fortified or balanced ration. If the food is not labeled "complete" do not feed it exclusively. However, it is all right to use it as a supplement. Whenever you see the word "complete" on a label of canned pet food it means the ration should sustain a dog without additional substances other than water. However, it is still wise to watch your dog's condition, as vitamin deficiencies have been known to occur when some brands of canned food were fed as the sole ration.

Canned foods are generally well received by animals, due in part to their meat-like texture, consistency and aroma. Canned foods have two disadvantages, however as far as the pet owner is concerned. 1. They are considerably more expensive than dry foods because they require thermal processing in sealed containers to obtain a commercially sterile product. 2. They must be consumed quickly or they will deteriorate rapidly unless stored in the refrigerator.

If you want to mix your own ration, using a combination of meal and canned meat, use 20 to 25 percent canned meat with dry food.

Be sure to mix the canned meat thoroughly with the dry food. This is recommended because some dogs will pick out the meat and leave the dry food. If your dog refuses to eat a combination of the two it may be necessary to introduce the dry food gradually. To start, add a few spoonfuls of dry food to the canned meat. Increase the amount each day until you are using the right percentage of canned meat with the dry food.

Fresh or Frozen Meat

As mentioned earlier, a meat-only diet is not the best possible diet for dogs. In the wild state, the dog does not eat meat alone, but eats the stomach and intestines of his prey, which supplies other nutrients, vitamins, minerals, and fiber to make a complete balanced diet.

Meat protein must be supplemented with the right amount of proteins from vegetables and grains. Fats, starches and sugars are needed to balance this out. When using meat to supplement a diet, beef and horse meat should be fed cooked. Pork should be well done and fish should also be cooked. Refer to Chapters 9 and 10 for the reasons why these foods must be cooked.

Now that you have become familiar with the descriptions of each of the commonly available commercial foods let's look at how much these foods cost. The following price breakdowns, of the most popular dog foods, show how much a daily ration costs for the various breeds from the very small to the very large.

It should be noted that the price of food will vary from location to location. Similar items may be purchased for less, sometimes for more. The purpose of the cost analysis given here is to familarize the pet owner with what is available and how the cost increases due to processing and packaging even though the nutritional value remains the same. For purposes of comparison, the cost of making a beef stew at home is also given here.

The directions on the packaging of most commercial pet foods usually indicate that the food is a complete balanced diet and that nothing needs to be added to enhance its nutritional value. As was pointed out earlier, even though you have carefully checked the label, and the manufacturer claims its product is nutritionally complete, this is not necessarily so. No matter what food is offered the buyer is well advised to watch and evaluate his dog's condition.

Pellets

Pellet or chunk-type dry food costs about $1.33 for five pounds. There are about 28 cups of food per five-pound package. Two cups of the pellets costs approximately 9¢. The following amounts, fed once daily, are recommended for the average pet.

Size	Daily Ration	Approximate Cost Per Day
Very Small	½ - 2 cups	2 - 9¢
Small	2 - 4 cups	9 - 18¢
Medium	4 - 6½ cups	18 - 30¢
Large	6½ - 10 cups	30 - 45¢
Very Large	10 - 15 cups	45 - 68¢

Meal

High protein dog meal costs $1.33 for five pounds. There are about 20 cups of meal per five-pound package. Two cups of meal costs approximately 13¢. For the average pet the following amounts, fed once daily, are recommended:

Size	Daily Ration	Approximate Cost Per Day
Very Small	½ - 2 cups	3 - 13¢
Small	2 - 3½ cups	13 - 23¢
Medium	3½ - 6 cups	23 - 39¢
Large	6 - 9 cups	39 - 59¢
Very Large	9 - 14 cups	59 - 91¢

Soft-Moist Burgers

Soft-moist burgers with cheese can be purchased 12 to

a package for $2.44. The cost per burger is about 20¢. The directions on the package state that two burgers plus water can be fed instead of one, one-pound can of dog food. Or, two burgers plus water can be fed instead of 2 cups of dry food.

One company claims a package of 12 burgers "Feeds your dog for 6 days." What they really mean is that one package of 12 burgers will feed a very small dog for six days. A medium-sized dog would require at least 24-34½ burgers, for proper maintenance, for a six day period.

If pet owners choose to feed burgers, according to package directions, the following amounts need to be fed once daily:

Size	Daily Ration	Approximate Cost Per Day
Very Small	1⅓ - 2 burgers	27 - 40¢
Small	2 - 4 burgers	40 - 80¢
Medium	4 - 5¾ burgers	80 - $1.15
Large	5¾ - 8 burgers	$1.15 - $1.60
Very Large	8 - 14⅔ burgers	$1.60 - $2.93

Complete Canned

A "complete" canned dinner costs about 43¢ for one pound. One feeding per day, of the following amounts, are recommended:

Size	Daily Ration	Approximate Cost Per Day
Very Small	⅔ - 1 can	29 - 43¢
Small	1 - 2 cans	43 - 86¢
Medium	2 - 2¾ cans	86 - $1.18
Large	2¾ - 4 cans	$1.18 - $1.72
Very Large	4 - 7⅓ cans	$1.72 - $3.15

Homemade Stew

Should you wish to prepare a stew yourself, to be used in place of burgers or canned food, or to supplement dry food, it can be made for about 20 to 30 cents per pound. This is not difficult to do if you follow the advice of the National Academy of Science's Research Council. It recommends that dogs get 20 to 25 percent of their calories from protein, 20 to 30 percent from fat, and the rest from carbohydrates. See Chapter 9 for more information on how to go about making your own ration.

Should you choose to feed a home ration, in place of commercial food, use the following chart as a guide to approximate cost. This particular ration costs 20¢ per pound to make.

Size	Daily Ration	Approximate Cost Per Day
Very Small	⅔ - 1 lb.	13 - 20¢
Small	1 - 2 lbs.	20 - 40¢
Medium	2 - 2¾ lbs.	40 - 55¢
Large	2¾ - 4 lbs.	55 - 80¢
Very Large	4 - 7½ lbs.	80 - $1.50

Price Comparison of Various Dog Foods for the Total Daily Ration

Size	Pellets	Meal	Soft-Moist Burgers	Complete Canned	Homemade Stew
Very Small	2 - 9¢	3 - 13¢	27 - 40¢	29 - 43¢	13 - 20¢
Small	9 - 18¢	13 - 23¢	40 - 80¢	43 - 86¢	20 - 40¢
Medium	18 - 30¢	23 - 39¢	80¢ - $1.15	86¢ - $1.18	40 - 55¢
Large	30 - 45¢	39 - 59¢	$1.15 - $1.60	$1.18 - $1.72	55 - 80¢
Very Large	45 - 68¢	59 - 91¢	$1.60 - $2.93	$1.72 - $3.15	80 - $1.50

The preceding price breakdown indicates that the consumer must pay a much higher price for the individually packaged burgers and canned dinners than for pellets or meal. For the money, pellets, according to this survey, are the best nutritive buy. They do not spoil after opening and are relatively cheap. To get the biggest saving buy in 25 or 50-pound bags. When feeding large breeds a small package costs about 30 percent more per pound than the 25-pound bag.

A medium-sized dog will consume 18-30¢ worth of pellets per day. Were you to choose a complete canned food in its place it would cost 86¢-$1.18 for the total daily ration. The canned food will cost 68-88¢ more per day than the dry food.

A small dog may not eat enough canned food to affect the budget; however, large dogs can become costly to keep when fed the amount of canned dinner they require. Fortunately, most people with large breeds do not rely solely on canned dog food for the total daily ration. It is primarily used as a supplement.

If you were to use a homemade ration to feed a medium-sized dog it would cost 40-55¢ per day. The homemade ration will cost 46-63¢ less per day than the commercially prepared canned ration. This is a substantial savings.

This breakdown also indicates that the least expensive way to add fiber and variety to the diet, through the use of meat, fish, cereals or vegetables, is by preparing a home ration.

Additive-Free Pet Foods

Several pet food manufacturers have recently introduced additive-free pet foods, apparently in response to a growing concern shown by pet owners as regards the possible serious effects of prolonged additive intake.

Numerous additives such as synthetic colors, synthetic flavors, sugar, salt, preservatives such as sodium
nitrate, sodium nitrite, BHA and BHT, are regularly
added to pet food. They are necessary to processing.
While they may appeal to the pet owner's sense of
smell, none is necessary for canine nutrition—indeed,
the long range harmful effect of these additives has not
been determined.

Artificial ingredients in commercial pet foods are
used to enhance attractiveness and to boost flavor.
Sodium nitrite and other preservatives are used to pro-
long shelf-life. These substances have nothing to do
with canine nutrition. Medical research has shown a
correlation between additive intake and hyperactivity in
children. If additive intake causes hyperactivity in children such a relationship may also exist in respect to
animals. Eventually, as was the case in infant foods,
consumer pressure may cause the pet food industry to
remove many of these questionably dangerous additives now present in pet foods.

The new additive-free pet foods come in two forms:
kibble and complete canned. As pointed out earlier in
this chapter, few firms, because of the high cost, manufacture kibble. It is approximately $1.99 for a five-pound
package whereas regular commercial pellets or meal
cost $1.33 for five pounds. The additive-free kibble,
which can be purchased at health food stores, costs
about $2.25 per five-pound package. One producer of
kibble with a wheat base states in its literature that pet
owners will feed 10-15 percent less kibble, by measure,
in comparison with the usual commercial expanded dog
foods.

A complete canned dinner that is additive-free costs
about 50¢ for one pound whereas regular canned food
for the same amount costs about 43¢ for one pound.

3. What to Feed a Dog

The basic elements needed by dogs are carbohydrates, proteins, fats, minerals and vitamins. As important as their presence in the food he eats, they must be available in the right proportions so that his digestive system can assimilate them to proper advantage. Fresh water should be available at all times and vitamin supplements used only when necessary.

For most people who own pets the simplest and most convenient way to feed a dog is with dry meal or pellets. However, there are pet owners whose pets prefer a homemade ration, which may consist of breakfast cereals mixed with ground meat, liver, fish or chicken and vegetables. Added to this are leftovers from the table. Recipes are provided at the back of this book for pet owners who prefer feeding by the latter method.

When large breeds are fed, home formulas can be less

expensive than leading brands of commercially prepared products. Foods prepared at home also provide more fiber and roughage than the store-bought product. If a freezer is available a month's supply of food can be prepared at one time and frozen in containers or plastic bags until ready for use. Each evening the next day's supply of food can be defrosted overnight in the refrigerator.

Refer to the individual chapters for specific information on what to feed and how to feed. Feeding utensils, special diets, and other problems are covered. Following is a discussion of the elements needed for adequate nourishment.

Carbohydrates

Carbohydrates are energy-producing foods derived from plants. They consist principally of cellulose, starch and sugars. Cellulose is not digestible by a dog; sugars are easily digested. Starches are best utilized when fed cooked.

The level of carbohydrates in dog food should compose approximately 50 percent of the dry weight of the diet. Keeping carbohydrates at this level assures that there is adequate room in the diet for protein, fat, vitamins and minerals.

Proteins

The amount of protein needed in the adult dog's daily diet is open to debate. Some veterinarians claim that any growing breed could probably get along on a diet which included 15 percent of complete protein, while an adult animal could probably get along on 4 to 6 percent. Then there is the other extreme—that raw meat should form 75 percent of the diet.

Meat is the most common source of protein fed to a

dog, however, it is not the only source. Plant proteins, eggs, and milk are other good sources. Proteins that contain all the essential amino acids are called complete. Examples are meat, eggs, milk, peanuts, and soy beans.

When meat is the sole source of protein in the home made diet it should constitute at least 25 percent of the weight of the mixture. It should be remembered that some dogs may have a slightly higher than normal protein requirement. And the nursing mother will require double the maintenance quantity of protein.

On the other hand, if you're adding meat to a commercial dog food, meat should constitute about 10 percent of the weight of the mixture. Too much meat will dilute commerical dog food to the extent that the diet will no longer be balanced.

Eggs, milk, cheese, cottage cheese and fish are all rich sources of protein. Egg protein is probably the best source of balanced amino acids for dogs. However, eggs should never be fed to a dog raw as they can cause a deficiency in the vitamin, biotin. In turn, a biotin deficiency can cause annoying skin conditions. Fish, too, should always be cooked. Some veterinarians flatly recommend cooking all meat because an enzyme found in raw meat and raw fish is known to destroy thiamine.

Fat

For the maintenance of normal health, some fat should be incorporated into a dog's diet. No minimum requirement has been established but it is usually safe to say that the amount consumed should be between 25 and 30 percent of the calories in the food. If fat exceeds this amount it could reduce food intake and thereby retard growth. When high-fat diets are fed, protein, minerals and vitamins need to be adjusted in the same proportion to maintain proper nutritional balance. It should also be kept in mind that a certain percentage of fat in the diet is necessary for the proper absorption of the fat-soluble vitamins—A, D, E, and K.

Minerals

Minerals are used by the body in many ways and in varying amounts. Although many have a known or possible role in nutrition and metabolism they yield no energy to the body.

The major minerals, calcium, phosphorus, potassium, magnesium and sodium should be present in the diet in adequate amounts and in the proper ratio. A good example of a balanced supplement is milk. Milk almost always carries the proper amount of calcium and the proper proportion of phosphorus to go with it.

If a mineral supplement such as bone meal is fed do not use an excessive amount: To do so will invarably lead to an imbalance in the mineral portion of the diet instead of correcting it. In fact, the use of supplements should be discouraged except as directed by a veterinarian, since it is possible to feed too many minerals, causing a toxic effect. Trace minerals are usually found in adequate amounts in natural ingredients.

Calcium	*Phosphorus*
bones	meat
bonemeal	fish
milk	bones
cheese	cereals
	milk
	cheese

Sodium
salt
blood

Chlorine
salt
blood

Potassium
potatoes
vegetables
blood

Magnesium
bones
vegetables

Iron
egg yolk
liver
kidney
heart
gizzard
bone marrow

Copper
blood
copper sulfate
copper carbonate

Cobalt
eggs
liver
organ meats
dairy foods

Zinc
natural ingredients
zinc oxide

Iodine
fish meal
shell fish
iodized salt

Manganese
vegetables
bones
manganese oxide
manganese carbonate

Vitamins

Vitamins are commonly divided into two groups depending on whether they will dissolve in oil or water. The fat-soluble vitamins are vitamins A, D, E, and K. Water-soluble vitamins are those that dissolve in water. They include the B-complex vitamins and vitamin C.

Vitamin poisoning is a serious threat to many dogs because concentrated vitamin supplements are readily available to any dog owner, and when over-consumed, these supplements can cause a toxic reaction.

Refer to the following list. It provides the major natural sources of vitamins for the dog.

Vitamin A
egg yolk
liver
fish liver oils
corn
glandular organs
dark green vegetables
milk

Vitamin C
fruits
vegetables

Vitamin D
egg yolk
fish liver oils
irradiated yeast

Vitamin E
egg yolk
cereal grains
corn
milk fat

Vitamin K
fish
liver
soy beans
yeast
riboflavin

Thiamine
liver
yeast
whole grains

Vitamin B
milk
yeast
whole grains

Niacin
meat
eggs
fish meal
whole grains
yeast

Pyridoxine
fish
liver
meat
milk
whole grains
yeast

Folic Acid
liver
yeast

Vitamin B12
fish meal
liver
meat
dairy foods

Pantothenic Acid
liver
rice
yeast
dairy foods

Biotin
most natural
  ingredients

Choline
meat
liver
eggs
plant foods

Water

There are several factors that affect the amount of water drunk daily by a dog. First, this amount will vary according to the amount of moisture present in his food. Dehydrated meals and biscuits contain approximately 7 percent water, while some canned foods and meat may contain 75 percent water. Dogs eating a diet high in dry foods will consume more water than dogs on a moister diet. For proper digestion and nutrient absorption, a dog will drink about one quart of water for every pound of dry food eaten. Drinking should be avoided immediately after meals as it may cause indigestion and bloating.

A reduction in the amount of food consumed may also result in a reduction of water consumption. The amount of salt in the diet, disease, active exercise, and temperature and humidity also affect the amount of water a dog drinks. Since excess water is readily eliminated it is unlikely that most dogs would drink too much water. Therefore, keep a pan of fresh, clean water available at all times. Water dishes should be placed in shady places and changed twice daily.

Vitamin Supplements

When an already adequate ration is being fed it is not necessary to add commercial vitamins and minerals. Pet owners have frequently been oversold on the value of many of these products. And the last thing most dogs need is a balanced vitamin supplement. Never offer them to a puppy either: You may upset his normal growth pattern.

It's unwise to assume that if a little of a certain vitamin is good, a lot would be better. To work effectively, vitamins and minerals must be in correct balance with one another. If an animal is deficient in one or two things, and you add a balanced supplement, the deficiency is still there but at a different level. This is because the need for everything goes up proportionately when one or two vitamins or minerals are added. What you want to do is change the proportions when an imbalance is suspected. Many pet owners do not understand this. They use supplements indiscriminately, and this can be harmful to the dog. Instead of dispensing supplements, analyze the diet with the help of a veterinarian and find out what is needed. Once the imbalance is corrected, however, eliminate the supplementation and change to a good balanced diet. Some pet owners add various oils, fatty acids, and other concoctions to a dog's food to improve coat luster. A balanced diet contains the elements needed for healthy skin and hair. A dull coat can be caused by other problems such as worms or external parasites.

For years, cod-liver oil and wheat germ oil have been a commonly used and acceptable supplement in dog feeding. But you have to be careful. If it goes rancid it can destroy vitamin E in both the food and in the body and cause reproductive failure. Adding excess cod-liver oil can supply more vitamin D than is needed by the dog. It is important that Vitamin D be given in the proper proportion along with calcium and phosphorus for good bone and tooth formation.

Supplementing Home Prepared Rations

Some pet owners and dog breeders supplement their own special rations with whole grains, flours, cereals, seaweed, oils and a wide variety of natural foodstuffs. They also use herbs and spices of all kinds including dried greens, dried fish and other dehydrated foods. Since these foodstuffs are nutrient-rich they should be used sparingly. Before adding any supplements to your specially prepared ration it is best to consult with your veterinarian. Also, some dogs may have allergic reactions to some foods.

Following is a list of ingredients found in health food stores and some pet supply stores that may be used in a home prepared ration (do not add these items to commercially prepared pet foods):

dried spinach	brown rice
dried fish	alfalfa sprouts
bone meal	soy beans
kelp powder	dried sea weed
dessicated liver powder	sesame paste
glandular organ powder	bran flakes
Brewers yeast	wheat germ

Leftovers from the Table

Table scraps may be added to your dog's food as long as they total no more than about 15 percent of the day's food. When leftovers exceed this amount the balance of nutrients in the remainder of his diet may be destroyed. Large quantities of leftovers can be stored in the freezer for future use. Cooked eggs, meats, vegetables, cereals, macaroni and potatoes can be fed.

Ice cream, candy, pastries and other sweet foods should be thrown out, not fed to the dog. Between-meal snacks of this type tend to destroy the appetite, as well as make beggars and nuisances out of dogs. Some dogs are so spoiled after getting a taste of something else that they will turn up their nose when their regular ration is placed in their dish.

Diet Foods

Diet foods which are sold only by prescription can be obtained through your veterinarian. Several brands are available. These foods have been specially prepared for dogs suffering from heart, kidney, intestinal and other ailments. Instructions for preparing your own dietary foods are given at the end of Chapter 7.

Undesirable Items

Ice cream, cake, candy and other sweet things are not the only undesirable items that dogs will eat. They'll chew, and sometimes eat, just about anything in sight. They'll eat grass, dirt, and even their own droppings.

One of the most common causes for dogs eating their own droppings is incomplete digestion, in the first place, of the food consumed, which passes out of the body in much the same way it went in. The dog, or frequently a puppy, is fed pieces too large for his digestive system to handle. It may also be due to feeding too much meat at one time. Or he may be infested with worms. A dog with hiccups generally has worms or indigestion.

4.   How to Feed a Dog

There are two accepted procedures for feeding adult dogs: scheduled meals and self-feeding. How each pet owner feeds his dog is a matter of personal preference. Most adult dogs are given one meal a day although some veterinarians advise two feedings. A light feeding in the morning coupled with an evening meal has two major advantages. It lessens the tendency of a dog to bolt his food and gorge himself. It reduces the likelihood of the dog to search for food away from home or in garbage cans. Hunting dogs or other pets release a great deal of energy over short periods of time and would also benefit from several daily feedings.

Animals fed this way are less likely to have digestive upsets from over-feedings, provided that the quantity of food is carefully regulated. Feeding a dog twice a day is also a good way to get variety into the diet. Of course, there is an exception to this rule. Puppies need to be fed more frequently since they need more food than adult dogs but are unable to digest as much food at one time.

Whatever the choice try to feed your pet in the same place at the same time each day. Never feed him off the floor or on the lawn in the yard. Dogs can be quite meticulous creatures and they will vacuum up filth, dead insects and anything else within tongue's reach. Avoid placing food near garbage bags or pails too; the ration may become contaminated with bacteria or parasites. Never place food on plastic bags, aluminum foil or paper towels. Pets have been known to consume these items along with the food. Pieces of foil or plastic may become lodged in the throat or intestines.

Dogs are basically creatures of habit and will respond more satisfactorily to a regular feeding schedule than to a system under which food is offered at odd times. Regularity at mealtime makes happy dogs—with steady appetites. Dogs have a remarkable sense of time and if you teach them to expect their food at a certain hour each day they will be less likely to make a nuisance begging all day long.

Pick a place for eating that is out of the way of foot traffic. Mealtimes should also be quiet. No sudden noises please; this may cause digestive disturbances. With a new or strange pet, it is always best to persuade him to come to you to eat of his own free will than to risk scaring him by making a sudden movement in his direction.

When offering a young puppy a meal, call his name, even though he is eagerly waiting for his dish of food to be set down. If his name is used whenever food is to be given, he will quickly learn to associate the sound of it with a treat in store and come running whenever called. This is a good way to begin obedience training. Use it to advantage as the foundation for any further training.

A good time to feed dogs is in the evening before your own meal. This helps to keep the dog from begging while you're eating. Evening is the most popular time for feeding because pet owners are usually rushing off to work or to school in the morning. However, people who are home all day may prefer to feed in the morning or at noon.

If a dog has been playing or exercising hard do not feed him. When a dog is hot and tired he rarely shows much interest in food. Give him a little time to relax and offer him a drink of water before feeding. Whenever food is combined with strenuous exercise a digestive upset may be in the offing. Likewise don't feed an animal before taking a long trip in an airplane or car.

Watch your pet at feeding time. If he cleans up his dish and begs for more let him have more. Should he leave part of his food give him less at the next feeding.

When adding a new food to the diet add it gradually. Do it by adding a little to a familiar food, gradually decreasing the latter until the new food is completely introduced. This method of changing over will prevent sudden digestive upsets.

There isn't a dog around that doesn't like to chew a bone. Bones are fine as long as they're large chunky bones. Chicken bones should not be given as they may splinter and puncture the throat or digestive tract. Pork chop and lamb chop bones are not recommended as they may break off in large pieces and become lodged in the throat. Bones can also become impacted in the intestines, causing serious complications and even death. Also, avoid sweet foods and raw eggs. Milk may cause diarrhea in some dogs.

A pampered dog causes special problems. He has been so spoiled by eating table scraps, or by holding out for choicer tidbits, that he won't eat the food placed in his dish. There is only one way to treat a fussy eater. Don't give in to him. Be firm. If a pampered pet walks away from his meal, remove the dish at once. Wait until his next regular feeding time and offer the food again. If he refuses, withdraw the food. The dog cannot stick his nose up in the air forever so don't panic. It won't be long before he's eating his regular diet with great relish.

A steady diet of top-grade dog food will make a better pet from the standpoint of health and temperament.

Different kinds of food are not necessary for different breeds. All dogs, from king size to the very smallest, require the same nutrients. Only the amount or number of feedings will vary. As an example, highly bred dogs, such as Toy Boston Terriers, may require up to three small feedings a day, rather than one large meal. Growing puppies need more food than a grown dog. The amount again depending upon the individual puppy and his rate of growth. See Chapter 6, "How to Feed a Puppy."

Feeding Bowl

Feeding containers can be purchased in a large number of materials. Those most frequently found for sale are made of plastic, stainless steel, aluminum, pottery and glass. Whatever your choice be certain it is non-toxic and non-corrosive. Out of those mentioned here, the most satisfactory all-round feeding bowl is the metal variety. They are light-weight and can be easily washed and stored without breaking.

Plastic bowls will also withstand considerable wear and tear, but can be reduced to a pile of rubber when chewed. Some dogs may swallow the pieces. Some plastics will crack or warp when subjected to extreme fluctuations in temperature. Pottery containers are readily chipped and cracked when handled carelessly. They are also heavy and difficult to store. Glass containers are unsatisfactory because they are easily broken.

The type of container you select will also depend on the length of your dog's ears and the shape of his face. If you have a short nosed dog you'll want a shallow dish. On the other hand, if you have a long nosed dog you'll need a deep dish. Should you have a Cocker Spaniel or other long eared dog you'll choose a dish with steep sides to help keep the ear flaps from drooping into the food or water.

Self-feeder

A self-feeder is a specially designed food container that dispenses food automatically. They are available at pet or feed stores in a variety of materials and sizes. Or, they can be made at home. Self-feeders hold about a week's supply of food. Dogs accustomed to self-feeding seldom overeat.

Dog feeders come in very handy if you have the type of animal that insists on pawing his dish or bucket until it's knocked over. Not only will the feeder keep the dog from spilling his water and wasting his food, but it will improve the sanitary conditons. If your dog's house or kennel is located under a stand of trees, falling leaves and insects can get to be a real problem. The feeder cover will prevent debris from falling into the food and contaminating the water.

If your dog is a little sloppy at mealtimes, or should you spill a little food or water, you might want to drill a few drain holes through the bottom of the feeder box to facilitate washing out the feeder. Don't paint the feeder though, or clean it out with pine scented sanitizing agents. Noxious chemicals and odors might affect the dog's nose and alter his eating habits.

Water Bowls

Most feeding bowls are suitable for holding water, as long as they hold enough for the animal to drink at will throughout the day. Some pet owners may prefer a bucket or pail for very large animals.

In hot weather it is most important for a dog to have water. Hunting dogs under the stress of work should have a chance to drink often to increase endurance and efficiency. A hunting dog should never have to wait until the end of the day to quench his thirst.

A diet that is too dry may cause high water consumption. Since the water content in foods varies greatly, it's advisable to supply too much rather than not enough water.

Automatic Waterer

Automatic waterers, like self-feeders, dispense automatically. Both devices have a regulatory gauge which monitors the level of food and/or water in the container. Pet owners, who have many dogs to feed at one time, find them convenient.

Measuring Cup

A kitchen measuring cup can be used to spoon out portions of dry or soaked food. Or, an ordinary tin can may be fashioned for use as a scoop. If you always measure your pet's food you can keep better track of his actual consumption rate. You can see that his ration is consistent from day to day. If he needs more you can control the increase. If he's getting too much you can cut back.

5.   Amounts to Feed a Dog

How often have you heard someone say, "My dog is not an ordinary dog" or, "he is an individual"? Probably many times. And it is true—all dogs are individuals. But when it comes to nutrition dogs are made the way they are by people. So when you hear people say "Spot won't eat this," or 'Bozo won't eat such-and-such food" it's because people made them that way.

When the children slip the dog something, of course, he isn't hungry later and won't eat his regular food. Many times the family gives the dog more than he should have—too many cookies, too many tidbits, too much exotic food. Most dogs will gobble up all kinds of scraps. Then, like children, they start begging for between-meal treats. In a very short time he'll get finicky —maybe even too fat. And the more you cater to his whims the more spoiled he becomes. If you eliminate the tidbits, feed a balanced diet, and put only the proper ration in the dish each day, the dog will be much happier (and so will the owner).

Dogs, like humans, should be fed as individuals. There are no absolute requirements that meet the needs of all dogs at all times. If your pet cleans up his dish with evident enjoyment, maintains his weight and keeps active, is good natured and playful, you can be quite sure that his food intake is about right. If he doesn't finish his meal you may have dished up too much. If he seems unsatisfied you may not have provided enough.

It's just a matter of using your judgment based on your pet's general appearance and his desire to want more or less food.

There is one problem that is run into over and over again and that is the pet owner's tendency to overfeed his dog. Some dogs will overeat if food is always in front of them. Hunting dogs will overeat, particularly in the spring, to replace energy burned during the gunning season. Or, they'll eat more to keep warm in cold weather. During periods of intensive training and hunting it is advisable to feed more heavily if they'll eat the increased ration.

Although some dogs are too thin, most are too fat. It is not at all surprising to see pets with a physique similar to their owners. This is so because people tend to feed their dogs as they do themselves or, they overfeed because they are bored. Treating their dogs to a snack is just a way of looking for something else to do—a way of trying to be good to someone.

Some researchers suspect that overfeeding may be a possible contributory cause of hip dysplasia. If the affliction is present, and you continue to overfeed, you may increase its severity.

An experienced pet owner will avoid feeding snacks

and adjust the quantity of food from time to time accord-ing to the dog's condition. Appetite is never a reliable guide as most dogs will overeat if given the opportunity. Age, breed, sex, weight, size, digestive efficiency, temperament, how hard the dog is worked and whether he lives outside or in a warm house are all factors that affect the quantity of food consumed. Several dogs of the same age, breed and size often vary noticeably in the amount of food they need.

The right amount of food to offer will vary, not only with individual dogs, but even those within a breed, strain or litter. Some dogs will stay thin no matter how much they eat. Others may turn to fat on half a normal ration. You must be the judge regarding a specific ani-mal's requirements. A dog should be lean, but without displaying his bones. His breath should be good and his coat clean and shiny. A healthy dog also has bright eyes, an alert expression and responses that are quick and eager.

During gestation the quantity of food should be increased to keep the female in good condition. After the puppies are born she will require twice as much food. During lactation let her eat all she can handle. See chap-ter 7 for more detailed information on gestation and lactation.

Substitutions

When supplementing other food for meal or pellets three ounces of cooked meat will take the place of about one ounce of meal or pellets. Five ounces of cooked green vegetables may also be substituted for one ounce of meal or pellets.

Avoid foods that are low in vitamins and valuable proteins. Good examples are pastas, refined cereals, white bread, crackers, rice and corn meal.

Measuring

When measuring meal or pellets remember that an eight ounce measuring cup, or a one-half pint container, will hold approximately five ounces of meal or six ounces of pellets.

Do Not Overfeed

Whenever possible try to follow the manufacturer's directions printed on the label. If the dog seems to be getting too much or not enough, increase or decrease the amount accordingly.

See previous section marked "substitutions." Remember, all-meat canned foods are not complete diets. They should be used only as supplements to a complete diet. Also note there are complete canned foods composed of cereals, vitamins, minerals and other ingredients which insure balanced nutrition. Chapter 2 gives additional information on commercially prepared dog food.

For a maintenance diet, some veterinarians recommend about ½ ounce of good, dry dog food per pound of body weight. Smaller dogs may need slightly more in order to stay in good body condition. Larger dogs usually require slightly less.

The following tables are broken down into breed, weight, daily caloric requirements, in round numbers, amount of dry food needed per day, with the cup measurement. An approximate amount for canned food, soft-moist burgers or homemade Meat Stew is also given.

The quantities given here are intended as suggestions. They're not inflexible amounts. You'll want to increase or lessen the ration according to your dog's condition. Should you want to combine one or more foods you'll have to vary the amount accordingly.

The breeds have been broken down into five groups according to the average weight of a mature dog. Your dog's breed will be listed in one of these groupings. If your dog is a mixed breed, select the group that best fits his size.

Very Small Breeds
(Adults)

Affenpinscher
Brussel Griffon
Chihuahua
Dachshund Miniature
English Toy Spaniel
Italian Greyhound
Japanese Toy Spaniel
Maltese
Mexican Hairless
Papillon

Pekingese
Pinscher Miniature
Pomeranian
Pug
Shih Tzu
Silky Terrier
Toy Manchester Terrier
Toy Poodle
Yorkshire Terrier

These breeds usually weigh five to fiteen pounds and require about 300-550 calories per day. Use ¾-1½ cups of meal or 1-1½ cups of pellets. For canned food use about 1 can daily. Or, use 1-2 soft-moist burgers. For homemade Meat Stew use about 1 pound.

Small Breeds
(Adults)

American Staffordshire Terrier
Australian Terrier
Beagle
Bedlington Terrier
Border Terrier
Boston Terrier
Cairn Terrier
Cardigan Welsh Corgi

Manchester Terrier
Miniature Poodle
Norwich Terrier
Penbroke Welsh Corgi
Schipperke
Schnauzer Miniature
Scottish Terrier
Sealyham Terrier

Cocker Spaniel
Dachshund
Dandie Dinmont Terrier
English Cocker Spaniel
Fox Terrier
French Bulldog
Irish Terrier
Lakeland Terrier
Lhasa Apso

Shetland Sheep Dog
Skye Terrier
Smooth Fox Terrier
Tibetan Terrier
Welsh Terrier
West Highland White Terrier
Whippet
Wirehaired Fox Terrier

These breeds usually weigh fifteen to thirty pounds and require about 575-925 calories per day. Use 1½-2½ cups of meal or 2-3 cups of pellets. For canned food use 1-2 cans daily. Or, use 2-4 soft-moist burgers. For home-made Meat Stew use 1-2 pounds.

Medium Breeds
(Adults)

Airedale Terrier
American Water Spaniel
Basenji
Basset Hound
Brittany Spaniel
Bulldog
Bull Terrier
Chow Chow
Clumber Spaniel
Dalmatian
English Springer Spaniel
Field Spaniel
Harrier

Kesshond
Kerry Blue Terrier
Norwegian Elkhound
Puli
Samoyed
Schnauzer Standard
Siberian Husky
Spitz
Springer Spaniel
Staffordshire Terrier
Sussex Spaniel
Welsh Springer Spaniel
Wirehaired Pointing Griffon

These breeds usually weigh thirty to fifty pounds and require about 950-1375 calories per day. Use 2½-3½ cups of meal or 3-4½ cups of pellets. For canned food use 2-3 cans daily. Or, use 4-6 soft-moist burgers. For homemade Meat Stew use 2-3 pounds.

Large Breeds
(Adults)

Afghan Hound
Alaskan Malamute
American Foxhound
Belgian Malinois Sheepdog
Belgian Sheepdog
Belgian Tervuren
Bernese Mountain Dog
Black and Tan Coonhound
Boxer
Briard
Chesapeake Bay Retriever
Collie
Curly Coated Retriever
Doberman Pinscher
English Foxhound
English Setter
Eskimo
Flat Coated Retriever
Fox Hound
German Shepherd
German Short Haired Pointer
German Wirehaired Pointer
Golden Retriever
Gordon Setter
Greyhound
Irish Setter
Irish Water Spaniel
Kuvasz
Labrador Retriever
Old English Sheepdog
Otterhound
Pointer
Rhodesian Ridgeback
Saluki
Schnauzer Giant
Standard Poodle
Weimaraner
Vizsla

These breeds usually weigh fifty to ninety pounds and require about 1,350-2,050 calories per day. Use 3½-5½ cups of meal or 4½-7 cups of pellets. For canned food use 3-4 cans daily. Or, use 6-8 soft-moist burgers. For homemade Meat Stew use abut 3-4 pounds.

Very Large Breeds
Adults

Bloodhound
Borzoi
Bovier des Flandres
Bull Mastiff
Great Dane
Great Pyrenees
Irish Wolfhound
Komondor
Mastiff
Newfoundland
Rottweiler
Saint Bernard
Scottish Deerhound

These breeds usually weigh ninety to one-hundred seventy-five pounds and require about 2,075-3,650 calories per day. Use 5-10 cups of meal or 7-12 cups of pellets. For canned food use 4-7 cans daily. Or, use 8-14 soft-moist burgers. For homemade Meat Stew use 4-7 pounds.

Tips on Feeding Dogs

1. Feed regularly and at the same time.
2. Do not overfeed.
3. When food is left over offer a smaller portion at the next feeding.
4. Unconsumed food should be removed within one half hour.
5. A dog that refuses to eat part of his food, or none at all, can be fasted for 24 hours. It is not unusual for dogs to refuse to eat for a day or two or eat just a small amount sometimes.
6. Food and water dishes should be washed frequently in hot soapy water. Rinse well.
7. Fresh clean water should be available at all times.
8. A dog with a persistently poor appetite may be ill. For a correct diagnosis consult your veterinarian.
9. Pets will eat almost anything including ice cream and ice cubes. However, these items are not recommended because anything icy cold arrives in the stomach in a lump and still chilled. A large serving may cause stomach cramps or nausea.
10. Highly seasoned and oversalted foods are not good for dogs.
11. Several small meals a day are better than one big meal.
12. Sloppy, soupy meals with excess liquid are hard to digest. Excess liquid dilutes the gastric juices and retards chemical functioning.

6.   How to Feed A Puppy

A new puppy coming into a new home can be frightening and cause some confusion. Be patient if his appetite is not too good at first. And whenever possible, it's also wise to check with the previous owner so you can continue with the original diet. Things will be a bit easier if the food is familiar.

For very young puppies food must be prepared that is palatable, easily swallowed without being chewed, and quickly digested. Should you change the food for some reason do it gradually because a sudden change may cause a temporary digestive upset and possible nutritional imbalances.

If a puppy is ill he may refuse to eat at all. Should this happen do not become unduly anxious. Forty-eight hours or so without food won't hurt him. If it goes beyond this time you may have to encourage him a little with a few teaspoons of glucose or honey dissolved in warm water. If this gets his appetite going he may take a little pureed food in a few hours. Once he begins to eat of his own accord you can be sure he's on the road to recovery. Just continue to keep him quiet and warm, and on easily digested foods until he can handle his regular diet.

Puppies are quite prone to developing violent attacks of diarrhea. There can be many causes: infection, parasites, excitement, heat, change of diet, diet deficiencies, raw meat or liver, too much food, or an allergy to milk.

Most puppies are worm-infested at birth. Just about weaning time they start passing them in the stool or vomiting up large roundworms. This is normal with puppies so don't think switching over to cow's milk caused the worms. Although it is of interest that as many as half of all mature dogs cannot properly utilize milk sugar (lactose).

If you're a pet owner, or breeder, who must feed puppies from the moment of birth you may be interested in learning more about the nursing period and bottle and tube feeding.

Nursing

A litter of new puppies should be watched carefully to see that they are all getting enough milk. Puppies just a few days old have been known to starve because they had difficulty nursing or were unable to nurse at all. Old animals that have had several litters of puppies can have teats so large that the pup will suck from the side or be unable to suck at all. If necessary, move the pups around until a satisfactory teat has been found for each one.

Newborn pups should instinctively find the source of food. Should they continue to have problems after fumbling once or twice you can help by gently opening their mouths and placing them on a nipple. You may also squeeze a few drops of milk from the nipple to help give them the idea.

You will have to watch closely to see that each puppy is nursing well and steadily gaining. A puppy that is getting an adequate supply of milk will have visibly swollen sides.

Puppies that are nursing satisfactorily don't need supplementary bottle feeding. Successful nursing works on a supply and demand basis. So don't rush in with bottles of prepared baby formula. Nature will always supply a hungry litter of puppies, but if you remove the demand, by bottle feeding, she will cut down on the supply. Remember too, no formula can duplicate nature's milk for essential nutrients or digestibility for the first three to six weeks of life.

Bottle Feeding

If a mother is unable to feed her young because of infected or insufficient milk, or won't feed them because she is nervous, they can be raised on bottle feeding. Commercial baby formula and bitch milk formulas are available and have been used successfully.

Your veterinarian will recommend the formula that he feels will be best for the litter of puppies. All formulas are similar, but not exactly alike. They vary in mineral content, protein composition and the blend of fats.

Home formula is less expensive than the ready-made variety. Should you prefer to make your own the following formulas can be used. Be certain to beat until all ingredients are well mixed. Store in the refrigerator. When needed warm only what you will use in one feeding.

Formula No. 1

1 cup evaporated milk
1 cup water
1 tablespoon corn oil
1 egg yolk
  pinch of salt
4 drops liquid vitamins
  used for children

Formula No. 2

1 cup evaporated milk
1 cup water
1 tablespoon corn syrup
1 egg yolk
4 drops cod liver oil
4 drops liquid vitamins
  used for children

Warm the formula to body temperature and place in nursing bottles similar to those used in feeding premature infants. If the nipple opening appears small do not enlarge it too much. Puppies will not nurse if the milk comes too quickly. A clogged nipple caused by undermixing or overheating the formula will also discourage the puppies from eating.

Sometimes eye droppers or doll-size nipples are necessary for puppies of very small breeds. Be sure all the pups are getting their fair share but do not overfeed or allow them to feed too rapidly. The recommended daily amount for a ten-ounce puppy of a breed of average size during the first week would be calculated as follows: Since the recommended caloric intake is 60 calories per pound of body weight per day, a 10-ounce (⅔ of a pound) puppy would need ⅔ of 60 or 40 calories.

When feeding from a bottle hold the puppy's body

parallel to the floor with the head slightly elevated. This will prevent the puppy from ingesting air. If a puppy's body is held vertically during feeding it makes it easy for milk to enter the lungs. Milk that flows into the lungs can cause pneumonia and even death.

If milk is refused check the temperature immediately. Milk five or six degrees off in either direction will inhibit sucking.

Tube Feeding

Tube, or "gavage" feeding, is sometimes used for premature pups, very weak ones, or orphaned puppies. Experienced dog breeders prefer this method if many pups have to be fed because it is easier and quicker than bottle feeding. It is the perfect solution in instances where a pup is too weak to suck.

Tube feeding is done with a narrow plastic tube similar to those used for premature infants. It is inserted into the stomach, and food which comes from a syringe at the other end of the tube is slowly released into the pup's stomach.

Never use this method unless it has first been demonstrated by a veterinarian, dog breeder, or someone else who is proficient in this technique.

The amount to feed will vary with the size of the pup. A slightly rounded stomach is a sign that enough food has been given. Be careful not to overfeed; only very small quantities are needed. A 4-ounce puppy needs about one teaspoon every two hours, an 8-ounce puppy, two teaspoons, and a 12-ounce puppy three teaspoons.

If tube feeding is the only source of feeding after birth, it will be needed every two hours around the clock for the first few days. Three or four hour intervals will be enough after that. Tube feeding is not advised if the puppy can be put with the mother to nurse.

First Solid Food

This may come as a surprise to some people but the mother provides her litter with their first solid food. She does this about three weeks after birth by eating food, partially digesting it, and then vomiting it before them. The mother's actions are probably purely hormonal so don't become alarmed if you witness this behavior. Let this be an indication that the pups are now ready to begin solids. When you make the transition do it gradually to avoid upsetting his rather inexperienced digestive tract.

A very young puppy will need a balanced food to supply him with all of the nutrients he needs to maintain good health and insure long life. Soft moist foods are excellent for weanlings.

Young puppies, especially prior to weaning, have been fed all kinds of things. A mixture of milk, baby cereal, vitamins, eggs and meat has been used by many pet owners. So has commercial dry dog food that has been moistened with milk, broth or water. If it is up to you to introduce the puppy to his first solid food, start him out by making a gruel.

Never add raw whole eggs to a puppy's diet. Raw egg white, if fed continually, can produce biotin deficiencies, which have been known to cause dermatitis, loss of hair and poor growth. Should eggs be added to the diet they must be cooked.

Other growing young puppies have been fed only lean meat. This should never be done. After being on an all-meat diet for only 3-4 weeks puppies can develop severe rickets. Small amounts of meat may be added to cereal or dry dog food. However, at this early age, supplementing with meat is not advisable as it may prove to be detrimental.

The daily intake of dry food for a growing puppy 8-9

weeks old, has been estimated at about 7½ percent of his body weight. If canned food is used his intake will be about 25 percent of his body weight. Puppies will consume more dried food if it is moistened. Stirring it well makes it easier to eat. Also be sure their food is moist during the time they are losing their deciduous teeth or they will have difficulty eating. Also, give him a rawhide toy or something else he can chew without swallowing, to relieve his itching gums. Some weight loss may occur at this time too so don't be overly concerned.

A growing puppy needs about two and a half times more food than a mature dog of the same weight. Puppies that have just been weaned need to be fed about every four hours four times a day. Some pups will do nicely on three feedings, others need five. Starting around the third month drop one feeding. And continue to feed three times a day until the puppy is six months old. Some puppies will eat the food as fast as they can swallow it; others take their time. If he hasn't finished within 20 minutes take the remaining food away and feed a lesser amount at the next scheduled feeding.

A word of caution should be injected here—don't overfeed! A fat puppy may be likely to go off his food at the age of about four months and become a fussy eater just when he needs a good appetite to encourage good development and sturdy growth. Recent research has shown that fat puppies grow up to be fat dogs.

From six months to a year most puppies do well on two feedings a day, once in the morning and once in the evening. Some puppies, by four months, have a stomach capacity large enough to be able to get along nicely with only two meals a day. After the puppy is a year old refer to the beginning of this book for additional instructions.

It is also wise to allow a lapse of about two hours between the last feeding and bedtime. And never give a semi-liquid food just before leaving him for the night. It will be difficult for the puppy to last until morning without relieving himself.

Start With Milk for Lapping

Teaching puppies to lap milk can be a distressing time for both pups and their owners. You will have to contend with sticky faces and chests, and sticky paws. And as they continue to splash and splutter in their milk they will take time out to lick themselves, and each other, spreading their stickiness all about.

Lap Milk

½ cup hot water
½ cup evaporated milk
1 teaspoon corn syrup

Combine hot water, evaporated milk and corn syrup, and have at room temperature before offering. Evaporated milk diluted with half water is recommended instead of cow milk to reduce the risk of diarrhea.

Some breeders recommend powdered milk rather than whole milk. However, fats are added to make up for the virtual absence of fat in dried milk. A mixture of warm milk and a little bacon grease or other cooking fats can be used. After several days of that diet the puppies are given a soupy mixture of milk, fat, and a commercial dog food. Pour the mixture into a flat pan three to four inches high. Small bread loaf pans are good for this. They cannot turn over easily and the pups won't stand in them. A small bread pan can handle one puppy at each end.

After introducing the puppy to lap milk he will be ready for a little cereal in his milk. Make a small amount of cream of rice cereal according to the package directions and add it to the lap milk.

Cereal with Lap Milk
For the Weaning Period

¼ cup cooked cream of rice cereal
1 cup of lap milk according to the
formula above

Serve the pups cereal with lap milk once a day for about one week. It is best to offer this meal at the same time each day before nursing. When the puppy is through let him nurse as usual for the rest of the day. After a few days let the puppy have whatever he can handle during one meal.

After a week of this the puppy is ready for a different food.

Cereal Meat Balls
For the Weaning Period

⅓ cup cooked cream of rice cereal
¼ cup cooked ground meat
lap milk

Combine cream of rice cereal with cooked ground meat. Add lap milk until the mixture is the consistency of mashed potatoes. Wet your fingers with cool water and make tiny meat balls the size of marbles. Offer these meatballs to your puppy. The new consistency will make the puppy a little reluctant in the beginning; however, it won't be long before they have all of these meat balls polished off.

You will want to serve these meatballs with your fingers the first time, but the next day drop them into their feeding dish. On the second day start feeding the Cereal Meat Balls twice daily. After about a week of this they should be able to handle three meals a day in addition to whatever milk they receive when nursing. Other puppies may need five meals a day. Water should be available at all times.

There is a reason for feeding in frequent small amounts as opposed to one or two large meals. Little pups sometimes think their next meal will be their last and often engorge themselves on large meals to the point of becoming ill from overeating. This ravenous appetite is usually present until 9-12 months of age. Let them have all the food they want during this period of rapid growth, but in small amounts throughout the day.

A correctly fed puppy is lively and playful, eats quickly with obvious enjoyment, then romps about and naps peacefully until his next meal. A puppy that is listless, dull and bloated is usually an overfed puppy. An exception to this would be a listless puppy with a condition called hypoglycemia, or low blood sugar.

Hypoglycemia is brought about by the demands of your puppy for a constant supply of energy which his body is not capable of meeting. Management of it requires that he be fed frequently during the day—perhaps as often as every three hours. In this manner he'll have a constant supply of energy to keep him bouncy and happy. As he matures you'll probably be able to reduce the number of feedings. Should your puppy fail to perk up, only to become listless again a few hours after eating, take him to your veterinarian. Diabetes is known to produce similar signs.

Right after weaning, to approximately five months of age, is the time when most pups grow fastest. Between 2-3 months of age they will consume the highest amount of food in proportion to their body weight than at any other time in their lives. As the puppy matures and gains weight, the amount of food intake in proportion to body weight gradually decreases and levels off.

When six weeks old or a little later, depending upon how readily the puppy has accepted Cereal Meat Balls, you will be ready to add a commercially prepared dry dog food to the diet. Most pups do not accept dry food readily so you will have to moisten it and mix it with some other food. Normally puppies will eat more if the ration is moist and mixed with meat or cottage cheese. Some pet food companies have specially prepared food for puppies.

Use the following chart as a guide to the recommended daily amount of dry food. It has been devised for pet owners who want to feed commercial food as the sole food in the diet. When other foods are added reduce the amount of dry food accordingly. Half the amount or less is all that is needed when dry food is mixed with cottage cheese and cooked meat. The amounts given on the chart are for meal, pellets, or a complete canned food—not all three.

Puppies
Feed 3-5 Times Daily
6 Weeks to 3 Months

	Meal	Pellets	Canned
Very Small Breeds	1-3 T	2-4 T	2-4 T
Small Breeds	3 T-⅓ Cup	⅓-½ Cup	3 T-⅓ Can
Medium Breeds	⅓-⅔ Cup	½-¾ Cup	⅓-½ Can
Large Breeds	½-1 Cup	¾-1¼ Cups	⅓-½ Can
Very Large Breeds	¾-1¼ Cups	1-1½ Cups	½-¾ Can

Never give a puppy dry meal or pellets for the first time unless it has been moistened and mixed with two parts of some other food. Coarse, dry food should be slowly introduced because it will provide too much roughage, too soon, into the pup's diet.

Three in One Dinner for Puppies Six Weeks or Older

1 part dry meal or pellets
1 part cooked ground meat
1 part cottage cheese, at
room temperature

approximate amount for one meal

2-3 tablespoons for Very Small Breeds
¼-⅓ cup for Small Breeds
⅓-⅔ cup for Medium Breeds
½-¾ cup for Large Breeds
¾-1½ cups for Very Large Breeds

Soak the dry meal or pellets in a small amount of hot water for about ten minutes. The mixture should be somewhat coarse, but not as soft as mashed potatoes. Add the cooked ground meat and cottage cheese to the moistened dog meal. Place the mixture in a clean pan and offer it to the pup. Remove any of the mixture that is not eaten and do not feed again until the next meal. Always give fresh food in clean pans.

As the puppy becomes used to this mixture you may gradually increase the quantity of dry meal as soon as he can handle the roughage. Once you find a diet a puppy thrives on, stick with it because frequent changes in food can cause digestive upsets. Never add any vitamin or mineral supplements unless your veterinarian advises you to do so. Supplements can cause toxic reactions. See chapter three for additional information.

How to Drop Feedings

Sometime between three and six months drop one of the daily meals. On this day be sure to increase each remaining feeding so the puppy is receiving the same total amount of food as he was the day before. Another feeding can be dropped after the sixth month. Just be sure to increase each remaining feeding as before.

As a puppy approaches the one year mark he should be doing nicely on only two meals a day, morning and evening. After a year he can get along on one regular feeding daily with a biscuit as a morning or noon snack. Some breeders and pet owners may prefer to feed an adult dog twice daily, on a permanent basis. See the beginning of chapter 4, "How to Feed a Dog" for reasons why adult dogs benefit from several daily feedings. As the puppy becomes bigger he will require more food. Once he has reached full growth, however, his daily intake should slack off and remain constant.

Scale

Pet owners that raise show dogs often use baby scales to weigh out portions of food. Scales are also used by professional breeders both to weigh dogs and to formulate diets. By weighing the animal at regular intervals the breeder can keep an accurate record of his dogs' nutritional state. When highly accurate records are kept the scales are used to weigh the food given to the dog, then to weigh the amount of food not eaten. If desired, great care can be taken to measure and weigh the exact quantity of each ingredient or supplement that goes into the animal's diet.

Bones for Chewing

Bones don't have much to offer in the way of nutritive

value but they give great pleasure to puppies and are also good for teething. Bone chewing aids the growth of permanent teeth and helps to loosen and shed the first ones. According to some veterinarians bone-chewing helps prevent or remove the tartar that causes tooth decay.

Puppies are particularly vulnerable to the excessive chewing and eating habit. Plastic toys, dishes, wood, sand and bones all tempt their teething gums. Dogs that are bored or confined will not only chew on these items but actually eat them.

The problem of chewing everything in sight can be prevented to a certain degree through discipline or by providing something to chew on or play with. Old shoes, hardwood sticks and toys made especially for dogs may help. Having dry dog food in a self-feeder pan where it can be reached at all times has been known to keep pets from looking for something to chew on.

Steak, chops, poultry and rabbit bones, because they can be easily cracked and splintered, should never be given either to a puppy or an adult dog. When the splinters are swallowed the sharp pieces may puncture the esophagus and pierce the stomach or intestinal tract. Bones that have been baked or cooked for a long time in liquids should also be avoided; these bones crumble and fall apart when chewed, and if swallowed, pieces of soft bones may cause constipation. Only large, tough bones such as beef knuckle or shank should be given to your pet.

Watch out for the puppy who insists on dragging bones all over the yard. Worm eggs can easily stick to bones and be licked off by the puppy, infecting him.

When a puppy discards a bone it can be saved for future enjoyment by rinsing it well in cold water and placing it in an oven until crisp and hard. Bones treated this way will last a long time and be readily accepted when offered to the puppy. If you would like an effective substitute that is safer than bones try rawhide toys, dry dog food or hard biscuits.

Emergency Rations

If you're unable to get to the supermarket or run out of dog food you'll have to concoct a ration from whatever is on hand in the cupboard. Many things can be used to meet such emergencies.

Try breaking up toasted bread in warm milk and let it soak for a few minutes. Then stir in some scrambled eggs or cottage cheese and any table scraps you may have.

Canned soups or fish can also be used. Warm slightly with a half can of milk and pour over shredded wheat, some other cereal, or toast. If you have some chunks of cheese on hand cut this up and add to the mixture. Oatmeal and evaporated milk can be used too.

Never give a puppy or adult dog any refined sweets, refined starches, foods that are highly sweetened, excessive salt or fats. The main objections to these foods is that they are rich in calories and contain nothing worthwhile. They may satisfy a dog's appetite but they are very low in vitamins and protein. They deprive your pet of nutrition and spoil his appetite for healthful foods.

There are often foods too that should be offered less frequently, and in small quantities, as they are low in vitamins and valuable proteins. Refined cereals, white bread, crackers, macaroni, rice and corn meal are good examples.

Tips on Feeding Puppies

1. Prepare a fresh meal for each feeding. Don't offer very hot or cold food as it may cause digestive upsets. Lukewarm meals are best.

2. Dry food strengthens and cleans teeth and gums.
3. Never offer a puppy small, sharp bones such as poultry or chop bones. They become splintery when chewed and may puncture the throat or intestines.
4. A puppy's diet is crucial during the first six months since his most rapid growth occurs at this time.
5. Leave a puppy undisturbed when he is eating his meals. Loud noises and sudden lunges frighten puppies.
6. Any change in diet should always be gradual. Start by replacing a small portion of his puppy diet with the new food. Increase the amount each day until the former food is completely replaced.
7. At the time you purchase your puppy be certain to get directions for feeding. A new puppy, entering a new home, should continue on the former owner's diet for a week or so while he is getting used to his new home.
8. Puppies like routine. Set up and follow a regular feeding schedule. Irregular feeding prevents proper digestion.
9. Feed three to five small meals a day. A puppy's little stomach cannot handle a large amount of food in one session.
10. Dry biscuits can be given as a morning or noon snack. Biscuits are crunchy and provide exercise for the teeth and gums.
11. A puppy's abdomen should be slightly rounded after each feeding, but not distended.
12. Sometime after three month's of age food should be mixed as recommended for adult dogs. However, still feed several times a day up to the first year.

7. Special Diets

Special or therapeutic diets, specially designed to meet the nutritional requirements of ailing or old animals, may be obtained through your veterinarian. These special diets, which are quite costly, are not recommended for healthy dogs. If your pet is suffering from heart, kidney or intestinal disease you may be interested in obtaining commercially prepared products, or making your own dietary foods according to the instructions at the end of this chapter.

Over supplementation of vitamins and minerals is a common cause of nutritional imbalances. Should a possible deficiency show up never treat it without first consulting a veterinarian.

The more common health problems will be covered here together with diet deficiencies and their symptoms. The information is helpful to dog owners with pets having special health requirements.

Allergies

Allergies can develop at any time and may affect some dogs seriously. A variety of symptoms accompanies allergic reactions such as sneezing, coughing, intense itching, rashes, diarrhea, local or generalized swelling of the body and inflamation of the eyes, ears, nose or throat. Allergens can cause a reaction whether applied to the skin, inhaled or consumed in food or drugs.

Some allergens, such as plant pollens, occur only seasonally. They may be bothersome one year but not the next if the dog is no longer sensitized to the pollens to which he is exposed. A good history of your pet will help the veterinarian in determining the allergin.

Dogs allergic to milk or other foods may experience diarrhea, vomiting, or both. Today, various tests, such as food elimination diets and skin tests can be given to identify the offending food.

If the animal's symptoms are chronic or constantly present they are usually caused by foods consumed regularly. Some foods may cause violent reactions while others cause less severe symptoms. You must know what ingredients go into your pet's rations before you can eliminate the offending food. This can be most difficult to do if the ration is constantly changed, or, even if the ration is solely one or two commercially marketed dry and canned foods. A considerable variety of foodstuffs, vitamin and mineral supplements and preservatives can be found in commercial rations making it troublesome to determine the specific offender. Additives and perservatives in commercial pet foods may cause allergic reactions in some dogs.

Veterinarians have observed that commercially prepared "high protein" dry foods and "high protein" canned foods may cause severe diarrhea in some animals. Raw egg white is liable to cause diarrhea too.

If changing foods doesn't help, your dog may have internal parasites or be a temperamental nervous animal. Or, activity could be the cause. Dogs which are racing up and down a run, or ones which are being exercised may be more prone to frequent elimination than dogs that are quiet or confined. Again it should be stressed that some dogs actually do better with one brand of dog food than with another.

Disease

Aside from injuries produced by external wounds, a perplexing number of symptoms may arise as a result of various diseases. Any one of them could denote several possible conditions. Be on the alert for anything that is not normal and seek immediate veterinary attention should any abnormality be suspected. Your veterinarian is the person best qualified to tell you whether your pet has contracted an infectious or non-infectious disease. Once the condition is isolated proper treatment and diet can be given.

Watch for the following: Lack of appetite, ravenous appetite without a gain in weight, loss of weight, bloating, constipation, diarrhea, restlessness, inertia, coughing, pain, irritability, nervousness, fever, shivering, runny nose, dry hot nose or watery eyes. These either alone or in a combination may point to the need of expert help to relieve.

Obesity

Nearly everyone overfeeds his pet. And almost every dog will eat about 20 percent more than his body requires. If an animal continues to eat more than his body can handle on a regular basis, he will become obese. Obesity is dangerous, as it shortens the lifespan of the animal, causes him to become sluggish, inactive and no longer playful. And paralysis freqently sets in as the dog grows older.

A dog which is properly fed will not become overweight. No dog can become overweight unless he eats more food than he needs. He will lose weight if he gets less food than he needs. It's wise, in cases of overweight, to cut out any meal-type foods, cereals and biscuits for a while, and feed meat, eggs, vegetables, cottage cheese, and skim milk instead.

Like people, some dogs have a tendency to gain more weight than others. Likewise as in people, the tendency toward obesity is often hereditary. On the other hand, there are some dogs, like people, who never get fat even though they are chronically overfed. This is because no two dogs or no two people utilize their food intake at exactly the same level.

Weigh your dog every now and then. If he is too fat, cut his rations in half until his weight is back to normal. Remember, when he begs for food, don't give in. In this instance you will have to exercise the will power to make him lose weight.

Under most circumstances, a dog that is fed all he can handle at each feeding, without becoming excessively lean or fat, is receiving the right amount of food. This is probably the easiest way to determine if you are feeding the right amount, rather than to follow a fixed pattern of feeding an exact amount.

Should an animal become overweight it will be necessary to place him on a limited food intake, on a daily basis, until a desirable weight is reached. It is preferable to keep a dog slightly lean. In this way he will be more active and usually tend to lead a longer, healthier life. When determining what you feel is a desirable weight, be sure to consider the size of the body framework. Some dogs are so shaggy or heavy-coated that it's really hard to determine whether or not they are too fat. The only way to tell is to bathe your dog. When his coat is sopping wet and clinging to him, run your hands over his ribs and hipbones. If you can feel or see them easily he's underweight and needs his ration increased.

A growing puppy should always be on the lean side because extra weight places too great a strain on the hips. If hip dysplasia is present, and you overfeed, you may increase its severity. The first growth impulse is bone formation. The impulse continues for about ten months, depending on breed. It is extremely important, therefore, to keep a growing puppy on the lean side during periods of rapid skeletal growth. Also note that puppies which are, slow to get on their feet, and make swimming motions trying to walk, may have rickets and not hip dysplasia.

Gestation and Lactation

The quantity of food needs to be increased during the gestation period. An undernourished mother may produce weak puppies with bone deficiencies or lack of disease-resistence. If the mother is too thin or undernourished her milk supply may be inadequate or non-existent. Food intake should be increased as body weight increases until about the last five weeks of gestation. During this time some animals have been known to have such a ravenous appetite that they increase their food intake by as much as 50 percent.

The reason she gets so hungry is that the puppies being carried by the female absorb all the nutrition she ingests. Then, after they are born, the female's milk furnishes all of the puppies' food. At that time she will eat a lot, so make sure she has all she can eat and then some.

As the animal's weight and food intake increases, divide and space the day's rations at more frequent intervals than before gestation. This is recommended because large meals may cause discomfort, especially in a small breed.

During the last weeks of gestation her interest in food may decline. Also note that some mothers may consume very little food for the first day or two after the litter is born.

No supplementation of any kind is necessary during gestation if a well-balanced diet has been fed consistently. You may hear ideas on the subject to the contrary; however, in most cases it is not required. See the latter part of Chapter 3 for further discussion.

Should it make you feel at ease to supply a supplement, offer a balanced food, such as pieces of cooked meat, poultry, or liver, cooked egg or evaporated milk. Some breeders recommend feeding a small amount of lightly cooked liver throughout the gestation period. However, the reasons the female benefits are not completely understood. Whatever the case, these additions should not represent more than 10 percent of the daily ration.

The frequent feeding practiced during late gestation should be continued during lactation. Fresh or evaporated milk should be fed between meals. She may eat as much as three times her normal amount, divided into small portions, spaced frequently throughout the day.

Some breeders recommend putting nursing animals on self-feeding as it eliminates worrying about how much food she needs. Fresh drinking water, milk and other liquids should always be available. Early weaning will prevent emaciation and loss of hair, both of which are commonly seen when a large litter nurses too long. Also, see the section related to nursing in Chapter 6.

Old Age

Elderly dogs should get the same ration they've had throughout their prime, except that the amount is decreased in keeping with their reduced requirements.

Older dogs cannot handle rich food supplements. Particularly heavy liver feeding, as it has a tendency to produce diarrhea.

Although the amount of nutrient requirements for older dogs are lower than those for growing puppies, both need high quality protein foods such as milk and meat. However, older dogs should be fed only enough protein to meet their metabolic needs, because excess protein is hard on the kidneys.

Diet Deficiencies
and Their Symptoms

The recognition and treatment of nutritional deficiencies can be most difficult because different levels of the same nutrient will produce different responses and degrees of response in dogs. And what frequently makes treatment complex is over-supplementation by the pet's owner. Should a deficiency be suspected it is best to consult a veterinarian for advice in regard to any dietary changes.

Some of the deficiencies that do occur are caused by overly concerned dog owners adding meat and eggs to an already balanced ration. This results in too much protein and a calcium deficiency. Too much fat in the diet causes another problem. The caloric needs are fulfilled before enough balanced food is consumed to provide the right amount of protein, vitamins and minerals.

The elements needed for adequate nourishment are covered in Chapter 3. Some typical health problems caused by nutrient imbalances are mentioned next.

Calcium and Phosphorus

An imbalance or deficiency in calcium and phosphorus will cause poor bone growth, rickets, bowed legs and other bone malformations in puppies. A diet high in lean meat is frequently responsible for a calcium deficiency. A deficiency causes osteomalacia in adults.

Potassium

Poor growth, restlessness, poor nerve development, poor muscle tone, and even paralysis may occur when diets are deficient in potassium. Potassium is usually found in adequate amounts in normal diets.

Sodium and Chlorine

An inadequate amount of sodium and chlorine can reduce the appetite and cause fatigue and exhaustion. Salt helps maintain proper fluid balance within the body. An excessive amount in dogs with heart problems can cause fluid to accumulate around the heart and within the body. Too much salt can also be hard on the kidneys.

Magnesium

Many abnormalities will be produced if a diet is deficient in magnesium. Calcium can be deposited in the heart and blood vessels when an insufficient amount of magnesium is present in the diet. The feet of puppies tend to be flat when magnesium is slightly deficient and nerve function can become impaired. A deficiency can also cause hyperirritability and convulsions.

Iodine

Iodized salt usually takes care of the dog's iodine needs. Large thyroids are caused, as in humans, by an iodine deficiency.

Iron

A deficiency of iron will result in anemia, fatigue and sometimes diarrhea. Some dogs may go through coat color changes when iron is not present in adequate amounts.

Copper and Cobalt

Anemia is caused by a deficiency of copper and cobalt. These minerals are important in forming good hemoglobin. An inadequate amount can cause bone weakness and fatigue. A lack of cobalt may impair reproduction.

Manganese

Not too much is understood about the deficiencies of manganese; however, it is involved with both bone growth and enzyme production and temperament in animals. A deficiency may impair reproduction.

Zinc

Zinc deficiencies are rare; however, zinc is necessary in small amounts for normal bone, muscle and skin growth. A zinc deficiency may cause skin disorders.

Vitamin A

Animals fed inadequate quantities of Vitamin A cannot see well at night. Deficiencies can cause deafness, large coarse skin lesions, dry skin with scaling and itching, loss of appetite, poor growth, complete reproductive failure, weak and infected eyes, and respiratory infections. When a deficiency is present there is also a tendency of the mucous membranes of the ears, mouth, digestive and urogenital tracts to have lowered resistance against infections.

Vitamin D

A severe deficiency of vitamin D will cause skeletal defects such as rickets, improperly calcified bones and irregular teeth. Excessive vitamin D may cause calcium to be deposited in abnormal places such as the heart, lungs, muscles and blood vessels. On the other hand, when there is a deficiency the body fails to assimilate calcium and phosphorus. Dogs have been known to die because excess quantities of vitamin D was added to their diet.

Vitamin E

Inadequate amounts of vitamin E can cause sterility in the female. The ova can become fertilized but the eggs apparently fail to become implanted in the uterus. Muscular and nerve degeneration has been linked with a vitamin E deficiency and so has abnormal lactation. All oil should be fresh and stored in the refrigerator after the container has been opened. Vitamin E is destroyed in rancid oil.

Vitamin K

The blood fails to clot properly if there is a deficiency in Vitamin K. Dogs are usually able to synthesize this vitamin in the digestive tract.

Thiamine, B_1

Thiamine deficiency can cause weight loss, loss of appetite and even convulsions. Never feed raw fish to a dog as it may produce thiamine deficiency. Failure of growth, nervous disorders, paralysis and impaired gastric secretion are associated with this deficiency.

Riboflavin, B_2

A deficiency causes growth failure in puppies, watery

bloodshot eyes, weakness, diarrhea, collapse, and sometimes death if an acute deficiency is present.

Niacin

A deficiency in niacin causes a condition called "black tongue." Dogs with this condition lose muscular coordination, slobber from the mouth, have bad breath, and suffer from inflamed looking gums and tongue. Black tongue is a disease similar to pellagra in man. Niacin deficiency may also cause nervous disorders, loss of appetite and emaciation.

Pyridoxine

Slow growth, anemia, nerve degeneration, loss of appetite, emaciation, convulsions and excitability are all symptoms of pyridoxine deficiency. Cereals, yeast, liver and meat are excellent sources of pyridoxine.

Panthothenic Acid

Discoloration of hair, depigmentation, hemorrhage, poor growth, erratic appetite, convulsions, collapse, and sometimes coma and death are caused by an acute pantothenic acid deficiency. Under normal conditions there is little chance for a deficiency of this type.

Choline

A deficiency of choline may cause deposits of fat in and around the liver, cirrhosis, and growth failure in puppies.

Folic Acid

A deficiency will reduce antibody production. An inadequate amount is also responsible for loss of appetite and growth failure in puppies.

Vitamin B12

A B12 deficiency can cause anemia, growth failure and reproductive disorders.

Vitamin C

Most dogs do not need vitamin C as it is synthesized in the liver; however, on rare occasions scurvy will show up in dogs with this deficiency. Dogs suffering from this problem will feel severe pain after remaining in a stationary condition for an extended period of time.

Homemade Dietary Foods

If your dog has had surgery, an accident, a food-related allergy, intestinal disability, or some other condition, your veterinarian may recommend a special diet. You may find commercially prepared diet foods somewhat higher in price than regular pet food. This is because they are scientifically formulated with special ingredients. The additional cost, over a nutritious regular pet food, will vary according to the dog's individual needs. In some instances it may be more economical to prepare your own ration.

The recipes that follow, which have been planned by animal nutrition specialists, may be used to feed an ailing dog. Let your veterinarian decide which special diet is needed and use the food according to his instructions.

Most dogs will accept these foods readily. If your pet, just introduced to the new ration, refuses to eat for more than two days, it may be necessary to start a program of gradual shift to the new food. To start, reduce the amount of his regular food by one-fourth. In its place add one-fourth of the new food recommended by your veterinarian. Increase the amount each day until the new food completely replaces the former food.

Allergy Diet

¼ lb. lean diced lamb
1 cup cooked rice
1½ teaspoons corn oil
1 teaspoon dicalcium phosphate
Balanced vitamin-mineral supplement
in a quantity specified by your
veterinarian.

Cook lamb thoroughly without adding seasoning. Add remaining ingredients and mix well. Store in covered container in refrigerator. Makes ⅔ lb.

Kidney Diet

¼ lb. lean ground beef
3 cups cooked rice
1 hard-boiled egg, finely chopped
3 slices white bread, crumbled
2 teaspoons dicalcium phosphate
Balanced vitamin-mineral supplement
in a quantity specified by your
veterinarian.

Cook beef thoroughly without seasoning. Add remaining ingredients and mix well. Store in covered container in refrigerator. Since the mixture is somewhat dry, it may be necessary to add a little water (not milk) to enhance its consistency. Makes 1¼ lbs.

Soft Bland Diet

½ cup Cream of Wheat
1 cup creamed cottage cheese
1 large hard-boiled egg

2 tablespoons dried brewers yeast
3 tablespoons sugar
1 tablespoon corn oil

Cook Cream of Wheat according to package directions. Cool. Stir in remaining ingredients and mix well. Store covered in refrigerator. Makes 1¾ lbs.

Low Salt Diet

¼ lb. lean ground beef
1 cup cooked rice
1 cup cooked corn kernels
1 tablespoon corn oil
½ teaspoon calcium carbonate
Balanced vitamin-mineral supplement in a quantity specified by your veterinarian.

Cook beef thoroughly without adding seasoning. Stir in remaining ingredients and mix well. Store in covered container in refrigerator. Makes 1 lb.

Reducing Diet

¼ lb. lean ground beef
½ cup cottage cheese, uncreamed
2 cups cooked carrots
2 cups cooked green beans

Cook beef until done. Pour off excess fat and cool. If canned carrots are used drain off all liquid. Cut carrots and green beans in small pieces. Stir in remaining ingredients and mix well. Do not add a vitamin-mineral supplement unless instructed to do so by your veterinarian. Store covered in your refrigerator. Makes 1¾ lbs.

8. Dry Foods and Fillers

Dry foods are cheap, easy to store, and not much trouble to prepare. These are some of the reasons why they are so popular. However, they have several disadvantages—they do not contain enough fat; when liquids are added they become mushy and pasty; and they may even stick to the roof of your dog's mouth when he eats them.

Although a dry food may be fed plain, it is preferable to add a moderate amount of fat and some all-meat dinner, stew, or leftover meat. Be sure to give your dog an adequate supply of fresh water too, so he can drink whenever he wants.

It is usually preferable to add animal protein to dry food rather than vegetable protein because there is a good chance that commercial dry food already contains a substantial amount of soy-bean meal, fish meal, wheat germ, dry skim milk, dried brewer's yeast, and sometimes cheese.

The animal protein in commercial foods is a combination of meat and meat by-products which have been processed at high temperatures to extract the fat content and then dried. The dry "meat meal" which results from this processing is not as nutritious as fresh meat because most of the vitamin B is destroyed by the heat used in processing and drying it. Chapter 2, "Commerical Dog Foods" provides more detailed information on dry foods.

Some people prefer to give dry food in a self-feeder. This method of feeding has one major advantage and that is most dogs will not overeat when fed this way. It is also simple and time-saving if you have a kennel and have to care for 20 to 50 animals at one time. Of course, what you serve will depend upon the tastes of the dog and his size. Big dogs need more filler foods—that is foods other than meats.

When any supplemental food is added to the regular diet you may want to mix it with water or broth before adding it to the customary food. When the meal has been moistened and mixed together it should be of a crumbly consistency rather than soupy. Don't turn the meal to mush either. Most dogs usually prefer it on the crisp side.

Dogs can be as individualistic as people when it comes to eating so don't become alarmed if they don't like certain foods or combinations of foods. Some dogs may not like vegetables; others may have difficulty digesting them, while other dogs, still, thrive on them. Eggs or milk may agree with one dog and cause upsets in another. Any of these problems can be handled with a little common-sense: Just eliminate the offending food if you find it makes him sick.

Check the dish when your pet is through feeding to be sure none of the moistened food has gotten packed down in the dish. The dog's hunger will not be satisfied if he cannot consume the packed food. And don't offer more than the dog can handle because it may go sour before it is all eaten.

Mixing Procedures
for
Dry and Canned Dog Food

Mixing together canned dog food and dry dog food makes a ration that most dogs will eat readily. The food mixture should be crumbly in texture. Just moist enough for eating but never sloppy.

Measure hot water into pan and add canned dog food. Mix to a uniform texture. Add dry dog food and mix until all of the dry food is moistened. You will need to add some melted or finely ground fat to the mixture. One part fat to four parts of dry food is about right.

Very Small Breeds

¼-½ cup hot water
  ¼ can all-meat or meat-by-products
  1 cup dry dog food
    melted or finely ground fat

Small Breeds

½-1 cup hot water
  ½ can all-meat or meat-by-products
  2 cups dry dog food
    melted or finely ground fat

Medium Breeds

¾-1½ cups hot water
  ¾ can all-meat or meat-by-products
  3 cups dry dog food
    melted or finely ground fat

Large Breeds

1-2 cups hot water
  1 can all-meat or meat-by-products
  4 cups dry dog food
    melted or finely ground fat

Very Large Breeds

1¼-2½ cups hot water
  1¼ cans all-meat or meat-by-products
  5 cups dry dog food
    melted or finely ground fat

Mixing Procedures
for
Dry Dog Food
With Crunch and Texture

Most dry dog food is specially formulated to be fed either dry or moistened. Some brands have better flavor and texture than others. It may be necessary to try several until you find one that your dog will accept regularly. If the food is not palatable, as may be the case with certain brands, your dog may refuse to eat it.

Some pet owners feed meal one week and pellets the next. While some feed pellets in the morning and meal in the evening and vice versa. The two may be alternated in any of a number of ways. Although made of basically the same ingredients, the pellets and meal are so different in form that a change from one to the other has been known to perk up lagging appetites in the same way as an actual change of diet.

For dogs which prefer their food moistened, with a little crunch and texture, about one part of warm water or broth may be mixed with four parts of dry food. It is preferable to use a warm liquid because it helps to release the aroma of the food.

Don't forget to add one part of fat to four parts of dry meal.

Mixing Procedures
for
Dog Meal
With a Soft Fluffy Texture

Some dry foods become a soft soggy mass when mixed with water. This is because cereal flakes have been added to the food during the manufacturing process. You may have to shop around until you find a food that appeals most to your dog.

To prepare dog meal with a fluffy texture you will have to use approximately one-half cup of hot water to one cup of meal. Mix thoroughly and let stand ten minutes. Stir once before offering. Always use hot water; this brings out the full appetizing flavor of the food as it softens the hard baked particles. If there are no cereal flakes in the food each piece of meal will retain its same shape and approximate size even though water is added.

Vary the amount of water used until the exact consistency that appeals most to your dog is obtained. Some animals prefer one part of water or more to one part of meal. Others want only enough water to make the food crumbly. Be sure to add one part of fat to four parts of dry food.

To add variety mix in moderate amounts of cooked green vegetables, fish or meat. Meat stock or gravy may be mixed with the meal from time to time.

How to Prepare Kibble

Kibble should always be soaked before being fed as it may cause painful bloating or indigestion.

You will have to find out for yourself just how much water or broth should be used because some brands of kibble absorb more moisture than others. A good starting point would be 1½ cups of fluid to 1 cup of kibble. Let the mixture soak for about ½ hour. If all of the fluid is absorbed then you have used the right amount of liquid.

If the kibble has not soaked long enough you can tell by breaking up one or two of the larger pieces. If the kibble is not wet all the way through add a little more liquid and soak the kibble for another 15 minutes before offering it to the dog. On the other hand, if the kibble is soaked and there's still some unabsorbed liquid in the dish, you're using too much.

Should you change the brand of kibble for some reason you may have to experiment again until you find the correct amount of liquid. Don't forget to add one part fat to four parts kibble.

Filler Foods
for Large Breeds

Whole wheat bread and cereals make worthwhile additions to the diets of large breeds. Wheat bread is a rich source of niacin and that's why it's recommended for use as part of the ration.

All breads and cereals that are whole grain, enriched, or restored are particularly good. This should include cooked cereals, ready-to-eat cereals, cornmeal, crackers, grits, macaroni, spaghetti, noodles, rice, rolled oats, and bulgar. Barley, soybeans and brown rice can also be used to extend the ration of a large breed. Be sure to mix with meat and fat to make the food palatable.

Potatoes, carrots, onions and green vegetables that have been cooked with a little oil or fat make good filler foods too. See Chapter 9, "Stews."

9. Stews

If you are feeding canned dog food on a regular basis just think what a financial savings to you and taste treat for your dog a homemade stew will be. The sample given here contains a flavorful combination of chunks of meat, vegetables, cereal, oil and seasonings. Your pet should find the natural flavor and aroma tempting. For a little extra crunch, mix some stew with dry dog food.

Palatability is a factor to be considered when preparing your dog's rations. Dogs enjoy a rich taste, chewy texture and an enticing aroma. Have you ever noticed how hard it is on a house dog, which is fed only once a day, to have to smell food being cooked for the family? He wanders around the kitchen and pesters you for something to eat. Well, it's the smell that's getting to him. So if you season his ration with onions, garlic and oil you're certain to excite and hold his appetite.

There is no need to go easy on the garlic either because most dogs like it so well they'll even eat the most worthless food, enthusiastically, if it is garlic-flavored.

It is preferable to steam all meat since steaming brings flavor out into the water. The meat broth can then be mixed, fat and all, with bread, cereal and vegetables. Also, it's not necessary to grind meat into hamburger because small chunks of meat are better digested than ground meat.

When you cook up a stew for your dog you can add broken dog biscuits to sop up the juices. You can also thicken the stew with rice or barley. Either one is a good alternate. Both should be thoroughly cooked however. After adding rice or barley to a stew you may want to continue to simmer it for 20 or 30 minutes longer to let the flavors blend. This is a good way to prepare stew for large breeds like Bloodhounds, Great Danes, Wolfhounds, and Saint Bernards.

You may be wondering which is better—to give your dog exactly the same food, day after day, or to vary the diet? Variety is preferable if a dog is accustomed to a variety of food. That way, when you travel, or run short of food you won't have to worry about stomach or bowel trouble when a new food is eaten. However, if a dog is accustomed to exactly the same food day after day, even the slightest change in his ration is liable to upset him.

Some people are reluctant to feed fish for fear the bones would stick in their dog's throat. Fishbones have been known to cause damage from time to time by sticking in the throat or between the teeth, but such occasions are rare. Whole fish, where the bones are embedded in the flesh, seldom do harm. Once swallowed, fishbones soften quickly in the stomach fluids. The dangerous thing is when a pet owner feeds a plate of fishbones left over from the family meal.

Bones subjected to the high temperature of the canning process, such as in canned salmon or tuna, are also harmless as the cooking reduces the bones to pulp. So don't be hesitant in feeding cooked fish, it's an excellent source of protein. Fish can frequently be purchased more cheaply than meat too.

Cooked fish is as valuable a source of protein as meat. Most dogs will accept the same kinds of fish eaten by humans. So if your dog likes these foods and they agree with him, they make a nice variation in his diet. Whole cooked fish, including the intestines, is better than fillet of fish. Dog breeders in Scandinavia use whole cooked fish as the main part of the dog's diet.

Research has shown that milk is as good for dogs as meat. It has more calcium than meat and more vitamins. It is considered by some breeders to be one of the very best dog foods. Should your dog or puppy appear to be sensitive to cow's milk you may have to switch to goat's milk. It contains smaller fat globules than cow's milk and is more easily digested.

Some pet owners also have the mistaken impression that cow's milk with the cream mixed in is just as nourishing for young puppies as their mother's milk. This is not true. Milk from a puppy's mother contains several times more fat and casein than cow's milk.

Another thing to remember is that when a puppy is weaned give him whole milk right from the bottle, unskimmed and undiluted. Never add water to whole milk; you would only be filling the puppy up on water.

It is all right to give a dog buttermilk and even sour milk. Most dogs enjoy them and they won't cause a stomach upset. Some veterinarians recommend giving buttermilk to dogs that are ill. Don't forget about cottage cheese. It has the same amount of high quality protein as lean meat but is lower in calories.

Never offer cold milk or ice cream to a dog because they are still thoroughly chilled by the time they reach the stomach. Icy cold food or liquids can even cause stomach cramps or nausea.

Dairy products may be used as part of the protein in the diet or to give added flavor. As you have probably noticed pet food manufacturers combine meat with eggs and cheese. Just don't go overboard on the protein.

Dogs will eat almost anything, even raw fruits and vegetables; among others, dogs will eat apples, pears, peaches, bananas, carrots, potatoes and turnips. Some dogs may not like certain vegetables; or some may cause digestive upsets. The troublesome ones usually are brussels sprouts, broccoli, beets, cabbage, cauliflower, corn, lima beans, peas, parsnips and turnips.

There is no need to avoid these foods just because they're listed here. Some are especially valuable as sources of vitamins and minerals and, if they are well cooked and mixed with other foods, such as cereals, meats, cheese, or other dairy foods, many dogs will accept them readily.

A good grade of finely ground alfalfa-leaf meal, one without large amounts of woody stems, is also recommended as an excellent vegetable for dog food. As for fruits, they do no harm but too little of them is digested to make them efficient dog foods.

Cereals, and some of their by-products, when cooked, make a worthwhile addition to dog food. Corn, wheat, barley, oats, soybeans and rice are all good sources of nutrients. Wheat cereal comes the closest to being a complete protein. Brown rice is preferable to polished rice. And whole grain breads can be used to good advantage.

As was shown in Chapter 2, commercially prepared soft-moist foods such as burgers and canned food can cost two times as much, or more, than a homemade soft-moist ration, which can be easily chopped and cooked. All the pet owner has to do is add a little seasoning, broth, or some other liquid until the right consistency is reached.

As an example let's calculate how much it would cost to make Beef Stew. According to what is recommended by The National Academy of Science's National Research Council dogs should get their calories as follows:

20-25 percent from protein
20-30 percent from fat
the rest from carbohydrates

This caloric requirement can be met using beef or other meat with a fat content of about 12 percent, and oil and carbohydrates as listed below.

Homemade Beef Stew

	Calories	
Beef	3,184	Calories of Protein
Beef fat	436	
Soy Oil	2,000	
	2,436	Calories of Fat
Onions	157	
Potatoes YAMS	837	
Sweet Potatoes	419	
Carrots	312	
Peas	331	
Lima Beans	926	
Oatmeal	3,538	
	6,520	Calories of Carbohydrate

The following quantities and seasonings were used to make 7, 14, and 21 lbs. respectively. The amount of food needed will vary with the size and type of breed. Refer to Chapter 5, "Amounts to Feed a Dog."

7 lbs. Homemade Beef Stew

1⅓ lbs. beef and beef by-products
⅓ cup soy oil
⅓ lb. onions
1 lb. potatoes
⅓ lb. sweet potatoes
⅔ lb. carrots
⅓ lb. peas
⅔ lb. lima beans
⅔ lb. oatmeal
⅔ tablespoon salt   SEAWEED
1 teaspoon garlic powder
1 teaspoon garlic salt
2 cloves garlic, crushed

14 lbs. Homemade Beef Stew

2⅔ lbs. beef and beef by products
⅔ cup soy oil
⅔ lb. onions
2 lbs. potatoes
2 lbs. sweet potatoes
1⅓ lbs. carrots
⅔ lb. peas
1⅓ lbs. lima beans
1⅓ lbs. oatmeal
1⅓ tablespoons salt   SEAWEED
2 teaspoons garlic powder
2 teaspoons garlic salt
2 - 4 large cloves of garlic, crushed

21 lbs. Homemade Beef Stew

4 lbs. beef and beef by-products
1 cup soy oil
1 lb. onions
3 lbs. potatoes
1 lb. sweet potatoes
2 lbs. carrots
1 lb. peas
2 lbs. lima beans
2 lbs. oatmeal
2 tablespoons salt   *SEAWEED*
1 tablespoon garlic powder
1 tablespoon garlic salt
4 - 6 large cloves garlic, crushed

It should be pointed out that it is more economical to make larger quantities of food. However, if a deep freeze is not available you will need to make a smaller amount.

If you prepare 21 lbs. of food you will need about a 15-quart container for mixing together the cooked ingredients. You may also want to put the onions, potatoes and carrots through a food grinder before cooking. And to facilitate handling, it is easiest to prepare the ration in five parts.

First; Cook the beef in half the oil until done. Set aside.

Second; Cook onions in remaining oil and a little water until tender. Add shredded or diced potatoes to onion mixture and cook until tender. Add only small quantities of water, only enough to keep the potatoes from burning or drying out. Set aside.

Third; Combine sweet potatoes and carrots, adding just enough water to cook until tender without making the mixture mushy. Set to the side.

Fourth; If frozen peas and lima beans are used, combine them and cook according to package directions. Set aside.

Fifth; Cook oatmeal according to directions and set aside.

Combine all ingredients in a large container, sprinkle in seasonings, and blend thoroughly. Or, if desired, you may add the seasonings to the various food mixtures while they are cooking. When the stew has cooled, store in plastic bags or containers and place in the refrigerator or deep freeze until ready for use. Food stored in the refrigerator should be slightly warmed before offering.

The 21-pound recipe, if packaged and frozen, is enough to supplement the dry ration of a large breed for 3 weeks. The author used this Beef Stew along with dry pellets, to feed a 70 pound Labrador Retriever. Four cups of pellets and 1 pound of soft-moist food made up the total daily ration.

The ingredients needed to make 21 pounds of Beef Stew, at the time of this writing, cost $5.95. This stew and others can be made for more or less money depending upon the ingredients used.

Fish Dinners

Fish may be prepared satisfactorily by any of the basic cooking methods of frying, baking, broiling, boiling, steaming or combining with other foods.

Most varieties of fresh fish are abundant and generally cost less per pound than other meats during certain seasons of the year. Frozen fish is sometimes less than fresh fish of the same kind.

Most fish is moderately priced and plentiful and has the additional advantage of being easy to prepare.

Fillet of fish is entirely edible and you won't have to worry about picking out the bones. Fillets are the sides of the fish that have been cut lengthwise away from the backbone. Frozen fillets may be cooked without thawing if additional cooking time is allowed.

To thaw fish leave overnight in the refrigerator. If faster thawing is necessary fish may be left at room temperature for 3 to 4 hours. To avoid any off tastes, care should be taken so that the fish flesh remains chilled at all times. It's not necessary to thaw until warm but only long enough to permit ease in preparation.

Don't overlook using canned fish; it's a familiar item in almost every home and on every supermarket shelf. Some varieties are quite economical. Canned fish is excellent nutritionally as well as easy to prepare. Certain styles and packs of canned fish cost more than others. For example, solid or chunk style fish is more costly than flaked or grated fish.

Many dogs enjoy eating fish patties or fish loaf. And a variety of things may be added to them to perk up the flavor. Try mixing together flaked fish with any of the following items that may appeal to your dog:

chopped or grated onion	white sauce
melted butter	creamed soup
fat or oil	steamed vegetables
toasted or dry bread cubes	mashed potatoes
grated cheese	cooked noodles or macaroni
hard-cooked eggs	soft bread cubes
evaporated milk	cottage cheese

Combine the ingredients of your choice and steam until cooked or heated through. For very large breads you may want to add some additional whole wheat toast or soft bread cubes, rice, or potatoes, and just enough milk to moisten.

Chicken Dinners

Ready-to-cook poultry is available chilled, frozen, whole or cut up, and comes in forms suitable for broiling, frying, roasting or stewing. Turkey, duck and goose are also well-liked by most dogs. However, some animals will refuse to eat poultry giblets of any kind. Canned poultry may also be used but it is generally more expensive than fresh or frozen poultry.

Poultry should be cooked thoroughly but not overcooked. The meat is more juicy and there is less shrinkage this way. Before offering poultry to any animal be certain to pick the meat away from the bones.

Most dogs will eat many combinations of poultry and many other foods. Try combining it with any of the following that might appeal to your dog:

cream soups	cheese sauce
cooked carrots	wheat toast
shredded cheese	bacon grease
cottage cheese	pan drippings
steamed vegetables	macaroni or soft bread
creamed vegetables	cornbread and evaporated
noodles or rice	milk
white sauce	

The remainder of this chapter contains a chart that lists some of the commonly available foodstuffs that can be used to compose a dog's ration. The caloric values given are for the edible portion of one pound of food as purchased. The caloric values have been taken from the United States Department of Agriculture publication entitled *Composition of Foods*. These caloric values are based on good or standard grades of food.

You may wish to experiment and make your own ration according to what foods are readily available in your area. Just remember, keep the ratio of proteins, fats and carbohydrates in proper balance. When selecting carbohydrates from the chart provided here keep a proper balance between green and yellow vegetables and cereal and other starches to avoid vitamin and mineral deficiencies.

Refer to Chapter 3 "What to Feed a Dog" for detailed information on vitamins and minerals. Chapter 8 covers diet deficiencies and their symptoms.

Approximate Caloric Value of Some Foods Fed to Pets

PROTEINS

	Calories Per Pound
Beef	
Carcass	1,009
Hamburger	812
Heart	1,148
Kidneys	590
Marrow	3,800
Suet	3,874
Brains	567
Fish	
Barracuda	513
Bass	445
Bonito	442
Butterfish	767
Carp	522
Cat fish	467
Cod	354
Haddock	358
Halibut	454
Jack Mackerel	649

King fish	476
Ling cod	381
Mackerel	866
Ocean Perch	431
Perch	535
Pickerel	381
Pike	408
Red Snapper	422
Salmon	984
Shad	771
Sword fish	535
Trout	1,093
Tuna	
Canned	1,306
Fresh	658
Whitefish	703
Horsemeat	427
Lamb	1,003
Liver	
Beef	635
Calf	635
Chicken	585
Pork	594
Lungs	
Beef	435
Calf	481
Lamb	467
Meat Loaf	907
Meat Stew	355
Pork	
Ham	1,397
Heart	513
Kidneys	481
Leg	1,397
Poultry	

Chicken	
Fryer	382
Hen	987
Rooster	791
Turkey	722
Tongue	
Beef	934
Calf	454
Lamb	659
Pork	741
Sheep	877
Veal	742

FATS

	Calories Per Pound
Butter	3,248
Lard	4,091
Margarine	3,266
Salad or cooking oil	4,010

CARBOHYDRATES

	Calories Per Pound
Asparagus	104
Avocados	568
Barley	1,583
Beans	
Brown	1,583
Garbanzo	1,633
Green, snap	118
Lima	463
Pinto	1,583

Soy	340
Yellow, snap	86
Beet greens	61
Bran	1,089
Bread	
Cracked wheat	1,193
French	1,315
Pumpernickel	1,116
White	1,220
Breadcrumbs	1,778
Bread stuffing mix	1,683
Broccoli	132
Brussel Sprouts	188
Buckwheat	1,520
Bulgar	1,627
Cabbage	98
Carrots	156
Cauliflower	122
Celery	58
Collards	181
Corn	
Bread	1,960
Cream	372
Flakes	1,150
Kernel	376
Meal	1,651
Corn grits	1,642
Cress	103
Dandelion greens	204
Eggplant	92
Endive	80
Farina	1,683
Kale	128
Kohlrabi	61

Lettuce	52
Macaroni	1,674
Mustard greens	98
Noodles	1,760
Oatmeal	1,769
Okra	140
Onions	157
Peas	331
Peas and carrots	249
Potatoes	279
Rice	
Brown	1,633
White	1,647
Spinach	118
Squash	
Summer	84
Winter	161
Sweet potatoes	419
Tomatoes	100
Tomato catsup	481
Tomato paste	372
Turnips	88
Turnip greens	127
Vegetables, mixed	295
Vegetable protein, canned	
Peanuts and soya	1,075
Wheat protein	494
Wheat protein and nuts	962
Wheat and soy	472
Watercress	79
Wheat germ	1,647
Wheat cereal	1,737
Yams	394

DAIRY PRODUCTS

	Calories Per Pound
Buttermilk	163
Cheeses	
Blue	1,669
Brick	1,678
Cheddar	1,805
Cottage	
Creamed	481
Uncreamed	390
Parmesan	1,783
Process cheese food	1,465
Process cheese spread	1,306
Swiss	1,678
American	1,678
Eggs	658
Milk	295
Evaporated	621
Dry, whole	2,277
Dry, skim	1,647
Yogurt	
Skim milk	227
Whole milk	281

10.   Meat Dinners

A dog will not grow healthy and strong on meat alone, no matter what anyone says, although he may contentedly eat it day after day and function well. Neither will he thrive on a 100 percent combination of meat and meat by-products. The truth of the matter is that if you feed him nothing but meat you'll starve him, or make him seriously ill, because all-meat was never intended to be a dog's sole diet.

All-meat was never intended to be a dog's sole diet because it deprives him of many essential nutrients. If you feed an all-meat diet you will cause a serious upset in the critical balance between calcium and phosphorus. When this interrelationship becomes abnormal a deficiency disease called rickets tends to develop.

Here's an exaggerated example to show you how this happens. A 40-pound dog would need to eat 80 pounds of beef every day to meet his calcium requirements. This much meat would provide him with twenty times his phosphorus need, so what calcium he did receive would pass through his digestive system unused. His body would try to make up for the shortage by taking it from his bones. This in turn would lead to brittle bones and loss of teeth.

A human being could never exist on a diet of all-meat so don't expect an animal to do any better. Dogs need essentially the same kinds of nutrients that people do—a balanced supply of proteins, fats, carbohydrates, vitamins and minerals.

Meat is not a maintenance ration; it is a supplement intended to be used with other foods. It wasn't until recent years that the Federal Trade Commission set guidelines for manufacturers, requiring them to indicate this clearly in ads and on labels. Somewhere on the product it will be identified either as a maintenance food or as a protein or pet food supplement.

When buying canned or frozen pet food don't let the term "meat by-products" fool you into thinking that these are the trimmings from meat for human consumption. Meat by-products have been known to include such things as gristle, hair, skin, pig's feet, hooves, tails, lung tissue, blood and many other things, although they all qualify as proteins, that cannot be transformed into nourishment by the dog. Other chopped meat by-products include such things as tripe, liver, udders, cheek trimmings, tongue trimmings, brain and gullets; however, although these may very well provide some nourishment.

Don't be fooled into thinking that dogs, if given a choice of foods, will always show a preference for meat. When equal amounts of meatballs, pieces of liver and stew (with small quantities of meat) were placed in separate parts on a dish in one experiment, the dog tested consumed the stew first, the meatballs next, and then the pieces of liver.

In this instance the preference was for a combination of vegetable and meat protein. Actually, this combination is better for the dog than meat alone. By eating the stew first, without any prompting, the animal gave silent testimony that he instinctively tried to balance his diet.

When it comes to balancing diets dogs instinctively have been known to eat almost anything from grass to the droppings of other animals. Dogs near bridle paths will even eat horse manure to obtain the partially digested grain it contains. It isn't likely to cause any harm. But you can be sure of one thing; a dog that satisfies his craving for carbohydrates this way is not getting enough cereal in his diet.

In the case of lactating dogs and hunting dogs the feeding of a small portion of fat or meat stimulates the dog to eat more. Supplementations of this type are recommended because these dogs need to eat more than the average pet dog to keep in peak form. If you improve the diet of a hunting dog you'll find he'll give you much more pleasure when you take him out. His alertness, pep and stamina will be greatly increased.

An active bird dog exerts a great deal of energy so be certain to increase the diet in accordance with the amount of work done. A bird dog should be in hard, lean condition during the hunting season, but not so thin as to appear emaciated.

Guard dogs that lead extremely strenuous and active lives while in training or on duty need large amounts of food to supply energy and maintain a healthy weight. As an example, let's look at what war dogs ate when they served with the armed forces in World War II.

The War Department's manual on war dogs gives the following as the daily diet for a 60-pound dog in training:

> ½ lb. cooked horse meat
> ¾ lb. raw horse meat
>   (ground with the bone)
> ½ lb. yellow cornmeal cooked
>   for two hours in horsemeat broth
> ½ lb. commercial dog food
>   salt added in amounts to make
>   1 per cent based on dry weight

This ration is certainly not recommended for a sedentary house dog as it contains far too many calories for a maintenance diet.

Dogs that are worked hard during the day herding sheep or cattle, or hunting, should be fed after the day's work is done. If you feed them early in the morning they are inclined to sluggishness throughout the day. To enable him to get over his excitement and stimulation, give the dog at least an hour to rest after strenuous exercise. Then feed him.

With a watchdog, you would have to do the reverse. If he is watching at night you should give him his big meal of the day in the morning instead of late afternoon. Dogs that have just been fed have a tendency to sleep more soundly after a large meal.

Excessive meat eating may cause bloating, bad breath and diarrhea. Too much meat in the diet may also overwhelm a dog's kidneys, eventually causing uremic poisoning. Some dogs, in particular older ones, cannot handle heavy liver feeding. It is too rich and oversupplementation has a tendency to produce diarrhea. If a dog is not accustomed to liver even small amounts can cause upsets. Also avoid feeding raw game such as venison; it often contains parasites. If you feed uncooked rabbit meat you are almost sure to infest your dog with tapeworm. Trichinosis can be contracted from eating raw pork. Raw lungs and udders may cause tuberculosis.

Straight meat, fish or chicken products give your dog variety in his meals and additional high protein nourishment. All-meat, all-chicken and all-fish foods, however, should not be relied upon as a complete dinner-in-a-dish meal. Always mix meat with a dry food such as meal or pellets, or add to a cereal filler or stew. Refer to Chapter 8 for additional information.

Now, as to how to serve meat—raw or cooked, ground or in chunks. A note of warning should be injected here: Feeding raw meat can transmit brucellosis to a dog which may result in abortions and sterility in breeding stock. (Brucellosis is also known as Bang's disease and undulant fever.) So be certain to take the time to cook the meat. Dogs raised on cooked meat frequently refuse raw meat because it smells and tastes strange to them.

Some veterinarians also recommend adding a little fat to the cooked meat. Fat helps keep the meat in the digestive tract longer for better utilization. And chunks of meat are preferable because when hastily gulped they do not pack down in the stomach and form a solid mass, as ground meat can.

When meat is offered in chunks some dogs have a tendency to pick out the pieces of meat and leave the cereal and vegetable portion of their ration. If your dog does this you'll have to change over to ground meat, which has been so thoroughly mixed with the rest of his food that he'll be unable to pick out the meat.

The nutritional value of meat from prime steers is almost the same as meat cut from old cows, bulls or horses except that there is usually less fat. Pork is difficult for dogs to digest and the fat in it often causes nausea.

Horse meat may be used in place of beef, but because it is so low in fat, suet or pan drippings should be added to it. Although pork and bacon are not recommended meats for dog feeding, bacon grease seems to agree with most dogs. Therefore, don't hesitate in using it as a way to supply fat in the diet. Approximately 1 to 1½ tablespoons of fat to the pound is about right.

If you don't happen to have meat drippings or other fat, use corn or vegetable oil. Use 1½ tablespoons for each pound of meat. Leftover butter is also good because it's rich in Vitamin A.

If you have never fed horse meat to a dog do not introduce it too abruptly into the diet. Mix a small portion of horse meat with a portion of beef, and then gradually increase the amount of horse meat a few ounces more each day until the changeover is complete.

Sometimes, local meat-packing firms will sell you lungs, tripe and udders as food for dogs. They are all right to use if they are properly prepared. Tripe is rather tough so cut it up into small pieces or grind it. Lungs are spongy so when buying them, purchase by weight rather than bulk as you may underfeed your dog.

A sick or convalescent dog who refuses to eat beef may eat a little well-cooked rabbit meat, chicken or turkey. During hot weather it's a good idea to reduce the quantity of food for healthy dogs as they may gain weight if kept on a full diet.

Many dogs appear to enjoy eating a variety of meats so don't hesitate to change the menu. For example, you could give your dog chunks of beef or horse meat two or three times a week, mixed with cereal, kibble, or dry dog food. Then you could use beef heart, beef kidney or pork kidney twice a week in place of beef or horse meat. The remaining two days you could give homemade stew, canned, or dry dog food.

Refer to Chapter 9, "Stews," for the chart that lists proteins that can be used to compose a dog's ration. It gives the approximate caloric value per pound, of meats, poultry and fish. A separate chart lists the caloric value per pound for dairy foods.

Savory Meat Dinners

Cut any meat that appeals to your dog into medium-sized chunks. For very small breeds you may have to cut the meat into small pieces. Use beef, horse meat, heart, kidneys, brains, lamb, liver, tongue or veal. The ration should be cooked slowly with onions, garlic, fat, salt and a little water until done.

Since the less tender cuts are primarily used for dog food they will have to be simmered slowly to retain the flavor and savoriness of the meat. For each pound of meat use:

> **1 onion, chopped**
> **1-2 cloves of garlic, chopped**
> **1½ tablespoons fat**
> **1 teaspoon salt**

If you like, you may extend the meat by combining it with broth, gravy, sauces, soups, stews, cereal, whole-wheat bread, biscuits, rice, or macaroni products, ready-to-eat cereals, bread crumbs, cornbread, potatoes, carrots and other steamed vegetables.

Mixing Procedures
for
Dry Food and Meat

Mixing together dry dog food and chunks of meat that you've prepared will make a tasty ration for your dog.

Measure hot water into a pan and add the meat. Mix until thoroughly blended. Stir in the dry food and some fat and mix until moistened. You can also add some cooked vegetables and a little cereal if you like. Use one part fat to four parts of dry food.

Very Small Breeds

¼-½ cup hot water
½ cup prepared meat
1 cup dry dog food
melted or finely ground fat

Small Breeds

½-1 cup hot water
1 cup prepared meat
2 cups dry dog food
melted or finely ground fat

Medium Breeds

¾-1½ cups hot water
1½ cups prepared meat
3 cups dry dog food
melted or finely ground fat

Large Breeds

1-2 cups hot water
  2 cups prepared meat
  4 cups dry dog food
    melted or finely ground fat

Very Large Breeds

1¼-2½ cups hot water
  2½ cups prepared meat
   5 cups dry dog food
    melted or finely ground fat

INDEX

Diet Sheet

Notes

Notes